Praise for *Leaders Ought to Know*

"Like Abraham Lincoln, Phillip Van Hooser has an easy ability to come up with simple but powerful stories from life to make his messages both clear and memorable. He is also remarkable in the way he brings out common-sense solutions to issues that his readers may already know deep down but somehow have overlooked as the best approach to their challenges. *Leaders Ought to Know* brings together Phil's lifetime studies in leadership along with his expertise as a master teacher."

—Dr. John Paling,
Former lecturer, Oxford University; Emmy-awarded
National Geographic wildlife photographer

"Blue Bell was looking for someone to impact our frontline supervision on topics ranging from employee motivation to hiring and leading others in a changing legal environment. Phil was able to deliver 'thought-provoking' presentations while allowing us to keep our unique corporate culture. Superb job, Phil."

—Greg A. Bridges,
Vice President of Operations, Blue Bell Creameries

"Phil's wonderful gift for insightful stories is on full display here. He brings the principles of great leadership to life with terrific examples that you will recall long after the last page is turned. Yes, *Leaders Ought to Know* and will know after finishing Phil's latest book!"

—Jay Akridge,
Glenn W. Sample Dean of Agriculture, Purdue University

"Leaders are not created overnight; rather, they are grown through experience, expertise, and energy. Phillip Van Hooser substantively and effectively explores the essentials of taking the helm of any organization through a modern, multimedia approach covering motivation, communication, change, and more. A must for any business executive."

—Dr. Nido Qubein,
President, High Point University; Chairman,
Great Harvest Bread Company

LEADERS OUGHT TO KNOW

11 Ground Rules *for* Common Sense Leadership

PHILLIP VAN HOOSER

Published by John Wiley & Sons, Inc., Hoboken, New Jersey.
Published simultaneously in Canada.

For general information about our other products and services, please contact our
Customer Care Department within the United States at (800) 762-2974, outside the
United States at (317) 572-3993 or fax (317) 572-4002.

Wiley publishes in a variety of print and electronic formats and by print-on-demand.
Some material included with standard print versions of this book may not be included
in e-books or in print-on-demand. If this book refers to media such as a CD or DVD
that is not included in the version you purchased, you may download this material at
http://booksupport.wiley.com. For more information about Wiley products, visit
www.wiley.com.

Library of Congress Cataloging-in-Publication Data:

Van Hooser, Phillip, 1957-
    Leaders ought to know : 11 ground rules for common sense leadership / Phillip
Van Hooser.
        pages cm
    Includes index.
    ISBN 978-1-118-52926-3 (cloth); ISBN 978-1-118-65178-0 (ebk);
    ISBN 978-1-118-65206-0 (ebk); ISBN 978-1-118-65211-4 (ebk)
    1. Leadership. I. Title.
HD57.7.V3645 2013
658.4'092–dc23

                                                                    2013001362

Printed in the United States of America

10 9 8 7 6 5 4 3 2 1

Contents

Acknowledgments   **xi**

Introduction   **1**
Can You Keep a Secret?   1
This Is a No Secret Zone   5
Ground Rules   7

1   Choosing to Lead   **11**
Born Leaders—The Myth   11
Your Most Important Professional Decision   14
If Japan Can, Why Can't We?   17
Congratulations, You've Been Promoted! Now What?   21
The Doctor Is in, and the Patient Is Waiting   23
Accepting the Challenge   27

2   Offer Service, Take Action   **31**
Management 101   31
The Four Management Functions   32
The Four Resources to Be Managed   33
If Not People, Who Then?   34
The Six Management Objectives   36
"What Do You Think?"   37

Mario and Luigi   40
Commonsense Leadership   44
The Ability to Offer Service   45
The Willingness to Take Action   47

3 The Essential Element   51
The Essential Element   51
Leadership Begins and Ends with Followers   53
Three Primary Assumptions   55
The Leadership Lie   60
How Close Is Too Close?   62
Know Your Followers   64
Who Are You?   66
Yes, and Then Some   69

4 A Recipe for Respect   73
WWYFS   73
Respect Is as Respect Does   76
The Recipe for Earning Respect   78
   Respect Ingredient #1: Consistency   *79*
   The Wisest Man in Princeton, Kentucky   *81*
   Respect Ingredient #2: Quality Decision Making   *84*
   "Honey, How Far?"   *84*
   Respect Ingredient #3: Interacting with Others   *87*
Wrapping It Up   90

5 Honesty and Other Truths   91
The Truth about Honesty   91
The Scheduler's Position   92
Leadership Failures   97

The Honesty Game 99
Game Contestants 99
Objectives of the Game 100
Rules of the Game 100
Losing the Game 102
Winning the Game 102
Time Frame of the Game 103
The Zipper Factor 103
Brutal Honesty 108

6 Two Motivational Truths 111
What Supervisors and Managers Want to Know 111
Help Me Motivate My People 112
Motivational Theories Abound 114
Motivational Truth #1 116
Motivation versus Manipulation 119
Manipulation Doesn't Pay—It Costs 122
Motivational Truth #2 124
Can We Have a Pool Table? 125
How Can They Sit There and Lie to Me Like That? 129
Is That All? 131

7 Why People Do What They Do 133
The Worst Motivational Speech 133
Giving before Getting 137
It's More than Gratitude 138
The Cornerstone Concept 139
What, Not Why 143
Determining Individual Needs 144

Easiest or Shortest   148

Preparing for Unsatisfied Needs   150

Emotional Defense Mechanisms   155

8   Preventive Leadership   157

Practicing PM   157

Embracing PL   158

Do Leaders Really Think?   160

Six Thought Processes to Support Preventive
Leadership   161

    Explorative Thought—Asking Why?   161

    Comparative Thought—Asking Why Not?   162

    Predictive Thought—Asking When?   163

    Creative Thought—Asking What If?   164

    Deliberative Thought—Asking How?   165

    Interactive Thought—Asking What Do You Think?   165

"I'm Moving to Alaska!"   166

Running from or to—and Why It's Important   171

The Wisdom of Dumb Questions   174

Dumb Question #1: How Am I Doing?   176

Dumb Question #2: What Have I Screwed
Up Lately?   176

Dumb Question #3: What Should I Be Doing Better?   177

Dumb Question #4: What Would You Like Me
to Do about That?   177

How It's Done   178

9   Fearsome Facts   181

Who's Your Daddy?   181

Understanding Fears   190

Fearsome Fact #1: We All Have Them   192

The Fear of Rejection 194

The Fear of Failure 195

The Fear of Success 196

"What Means 'Nervous'?" 197

Fearsome Fact #2: Unfamiliar Experiences Are
Breeding Grounds for New Fears 199

Making Unknowns Known 201

Fearsome Fact #3: Unsuccessful Experiences
Compound Our Fears 203

What It Means 205

10 Leadership Pitfalls 207

Seven Deadly Sins 207

Leadership Pitfall #1: An Elevated Sense of
Self-Importance 209

"I Hope the Old Man Is Getting Some of This" 210

Leadership Pitfall #2: Practicing Favoritism 213

"I'd Rather Be Flat Broke" 216

Leadership Pitfall #3: Inability or Unwillingness
to Control Emotions 219

When You Lose Your Temper 221

The Power of an Apology 228

Pursuing Leadership Success 229

11 Commonsense Success 231

Seniority, Experience, or Something Else? 231

Choosing Success 233

Too Many Choices? 234

A Professional Triple Threat 236

Knowledge and Understanding 236

Skills and Application 237

Personal Desire and Commitment 238

Contents

"I Should've Bought That Farm" 240

Commonsense Success Choice #1: If I Am to Fail,
   I Choose to Fail Aggressively 240

Commonsense Success Choice #2: To Hit a
   Home Run, I Must Swing the Bat 242

Commonsense Success Choice #3: Choosing Yes 245

Commonsense Success Choice #4: When
   I Mess Up, I Must Fess Up—Quickly 250

One More Foundational Concept 254

Conclusion **257**

A Conclusion Isn't a Conclusion 257

Congratulations to You 258

Leaders Are Readers—or Are They? 259

Leaders Are Doers—or Should Be 260

"I Wish Buster Was Here" 262

Acknowledgments

This book has been more than a quarter century in the making. As I reflect back, it seems my entire adult life has been focused on capturing, processing, practicing, and sharing the leadership information contained in the following pages. And while I wrote the book—it's my name on the cover—there are so many others who share direct or indirect responsibility for its publication that to not name them would be a travesty. Though I realize many readers skip the Acknowledgments section of a book, I can't. There are just too many people who deserve recognition, and I want to acknowledge them here.

It's a real honor to have this second opportunity to produce a book with the capable professionals at John Wiley & Sons in Hoboken, New Jersey. Wiley folks are truly a team, with many, many individuals playing a role of some sort in bringing this book to you. I have appreciated and benefited from the advice and enthusiastic assurances offered by senior editorial assistant Lydia Dimitriadis, senior production editor Deborah Schindlar, marketing manager Peter Knox, and publicist Amy Packard.

This project was initiated during a friendly exchange with Wiley Vice President and Publisher Matt Holt in an Indianapolis hotel lobby during the summer of 2012. That one conversation was all it took to get the ball rolling on what would quickly become *Leaders Ought to Know,* the book. From then until now, Matt has been solidly behind the project, never wavering in his support. Matt's a good dude and quite the snappy dresser, sort of Southern California chic.

Lauren Murphy, my Wiley editor for this project, has become a new friend and a real joy to work with as well. Her enthusiasm and support for this book project was evident from our first shared cab ride and the impromptu strategy session that followed at the Indianapolis Airport. I think we've made a pretty good team. I'm hoping this will be the first of several book projects we will have the opportunity to work on together.

My Wiley development editor for *Leaders Ought to Know* was Christine Moore. Christine was the first person outside my office to read the book draft, chapter by chapter. Her prompt responses with suggested edits made the finished book better in so many ways. I especially appreciated getting e-mails from Christine saying how much she loved this particular story or how a specific point resonated with her. Christine provided the technical inspiration I needed from the first chapter to the last.

The subject of this book, personal leadership excellence, was more modeled than taught by two of the best leaders I've ever had the good fortune to know or work with. Jerry Brenda and Art Malek were my earliest mentors during the dawning of my career, and they remain so to this very day. I appreciate the faith they showed in this very young, very inexperienced human resources supervisor, all the way back in 1980. It's a blessing that we're all still great friends today.

Acknowledgments

Tom Alexander and Frank Carmody, then both corporate human resources professionals at Emergency One, Ocala, Florida, provided the first comprehensive opportunity for me to share my emerging leadership concepts within the framework of a major organization. That was in 1988. Today, more than 900 other companies and organizations around the world have followed their lead. I thank them both, but especially Tom, for being my biggest cheerleader for a full quarter century.

As you read this book and the stories contained in it, you will meet a significant number of people who helped me shape my leadership approach in one way or another over the years. Most of their names have been changed in the stories for various reasons. However, I definitely know who they are—and I'm grateful to each one.

This is the third time my good friends, Joe and Karen Owen, have rolled out the welcome mat, making available their beautiful lake house on the shores of Kentucky Lake for my extended writing sessions. I couldn't have been more comfortable with the location, and I couldn't be more blessed to have such hospitable friends. I appreciate them both so much.

My wife, Susan, has been a constant source of encouragement for more than 27 years of marriage and for more than 25 years of business partnership. She has listened to and read each story, illustration, point, and perspective in this book more times than she could ever count. Yet her support for this project has never dimmed or faltered. Her loving, although not too subtle nudges to "write the leadership book" proved to be significant motivation to move me toward this finish line. I love her and appreciate her more than she will ever know.

I also want to acknowledge my children—Joe, Sarah, and Sophie. I've tried to practice solid leadership principles for them to witness and emulate. Unfortunately, I have failed more times than I care to consider. However, I trust they know that I will never fail to love and be honest with them. My leadership commitment to them is one that will never expire.

Finally, to all the folks who have ever voluntarily chosen to follow my lead. What an honor you bestowed on me! You taught me so much about practical, commonsense leadership and, in the process, we were able to do important work. I will always be grateful to you.

LEADERS
OUGHT
TO KNOW

Introduction

Can You Keep a Secret?

I was in Minneapolis, Minnesota, participating in a weekend retreat, along with 60 fellow professional speaking colleagues from around North America. The event was sponsored by the National Speakers Association, a group of which we were all longtime members. Various speaking experts—keynoters, workshop leaders, and trainers—were assembled, each of whom was a recognized authority in some topical category such as sales, information technology, motivation, leadership, or customer service. The group also included highly accomplished individuals who made their living on stages around the world in their respective roles as futurists, humorists, hypnotists, mentalists, and magicians. We'd all come together to share professional perspectives and techniques with one another, expecting to depart better prepared to share our skills and knowledge with our clients and audiences.

On Saturday evening, the group gathered for a night of fellowship and entertainment. We had the special treat of watching one of our own in action. A colleague who had spent more than three decades on stage—much of that time along the Las Vegas strip performing his highly acclaimed mentalist act—was set to amaze and confound us. It was a command performance before a very discerning audience. I intentionally found a seat in the front row to better enjoy the show; however, I never anticipated that I would soon be a part of it.

As my colleague began his routine, he asked for two helpers from the audience. I glanced around the room trying to guess who might volunteer, because I knew it certainly wasn't going to be me. However, before I knew what was happening, he was beckoning me to come forward. Reluctantly, I and a woman joined him on stage.

The first thing he asked of us was to blindfold him, and we took our assignment seriously. With that task complete, the show began in earnest. Over the next several minutes, this gentleman used the two of us masterfully as he set up and performed tricks that defied explanation. I can't speak for the lady, but I will say definitively that I was not in on it in any way. I had not been prepped or coached at any time. I was simply enjoying the show as a spectator from a unique vantage point.

Eventually, my mentalist friend sent me out into the audience in search of a watch with a second hand. Upon finding one, he had me pull out the stem and reset the watch to a time of my choosing. I did as I was asked. From a distance across the room—with me standing surrounded by my colleagues—this gentleman (who was still completely blindfolded) told me the correct adjusted time on the watch. It was amazing and confounding. Then, to add intrigue to mystery, he had me do it again—just to prove he could—and he was right again.

2

The audience loved it—and I was astounded. And even though he moved on to his next trick, I couldn't move on—or forget what had just happened. I wanted to know how he'd been able to do what he did. And try as I might, I simply couldn't figure it out. Despite all the thought and reasoning I could muster, a logical solution never presented itself. It remained a true mystery to me—which only led me to think about it more and more.

My confusion didn't end when the show did. I awoke in the middle of that night with that trick still on my mind, as well as the lingering question: *How did he do it?*

The next morning, I ran into another retreat attendee on my way to breakfast—a dear friend who happened to be a master magician.

Of course! Why didn't I think of this before? I wondered. *Leo's a magician. He knows all the tricks. He'll be able to tell me how this watch trick works.*

"Leo, what did you think of the performance last night?" I asked casually to begin.

"Phil, he was amazing as usual," Leo responded with great enthusiasm. "I've watched him work dozens of times over the years, but none better than last night. When I was a kid just getting started in magic, he was my hero. Now, all these many years later, I count him as both a friend and mentor. How cool is that?" Then, as an afterthought, he teased, "By the way, Phil, you aren't the best-looking magician's helper I've ever seen, but you did pretty good last night, too."

"Gee, thanks," I said. "But, I'm not quite ready to give up my day job."

We both laughed. Then I continued my quest for trick deconstruction.

"Leo, seriously, I have a question for you."

"Sure, Phil, what is it?"

"You know that watch bit last night?"

"Yes?"

"Well, I've got to admit that I'm still completely baffled by it. I couldn't understand how he did it during the show—and worse still, I was awake half the night trying to figure it out."

Leo's eyes were bright and completely locked on mine. His face was full of expression—the look of joy and wonder one finds displayed on a child's face on Christmas morning upon first discovering Santa's handiwork. He was undoubtedly enjoying my confusion, possibly imagining the same reaction he himself had created within minds of audience members, time and again, in countless performances around the world.

"Leo, you do know how that trick works, right?" I asked directly.

Leo moved his face close to mine. His eyes were wide, his smile huge.

"Yes, I do," he admitted breathlessly with a slight chuckle, all the while nodding his head vigorously.

"Leo, I'd sure appreciate it if you'd explain it to me."

Leo paused ever so briefly before moving closer still. Grasping my shoulders with his hands and leaning in, he positioned his mouth very near my right ear.

"Phil, can you keep a secret?" he whispered softly into my ear.

"Of course, of course, I can," I responded, in anticipation of the explanation to follow.

"Well," he whispered mysteriously, "so can I."

He then released his grip and stepped back, that huge grin still fixed on his face.

This Is a No Secret Zone

It's been about five years since I saw that show, and I still don't know how the trick worked. And frankly, I've come to the conclusion that I don't want to know. I've decided there needs to be a little mystery in my life. As for Leo's unexpected response to my question, I certainly don't blame him for being unwilling to expose the secrets of his mysterious trade.

On the other hand, it makes me consider the secrets of my trade—personal leadership development. And honestly, I cannot seem to find a good reason for concealing the proven concepts, methods, techniques, and processes that can inform and enlighten people genuinely wishing and working to improve their leadership skills and position. That's why I wrote this book—to unleash the amazing power that leadership represents, while eliminating the unnecessary mystery—the secrets—surrounding it. I wrote this book to help people in their personal quest to become better leaders—people like you.

For too many years—and for reasons beyond my capability to understand or explain—a select group of managers and supervisors have acted as though they needed to protect and obscure the mysteries of leadership from public view—as though they're tricks locked away in a magician's trunk. Many resist up close inspection; they reason that the art of leadership is like a vapor, virtually impossible to understand or master since it takes on various forms under different circumstances. These shortsighted individuals claim that either people are born as leaders or they're not; therefore, individual attempts to develop leadership skills are little more than smoke and mirrors.

I'm here to refute these false claims entirely and to encourage you. True leadership is not sleight-of-hand trickery. To become an effective leader doesn't require knowledge of a secret handshake to gain admittance to the leadership club. Leadership is not something to be withheld from some and bestowed on a few, anointing the chosen ones with some sort of magical leadership foo-foo dust. The act of learning to lead is actually the practical exercise of commonsense processes—a series of choices designed to influence and impact the relationship between you and others at work, at home, wherever.

In the pages that follow, you will discover a finely crafted methodology. My goal is simple: I wish to help anyone and everyone who wants my help to build a sustainable leadership approach that works. Period.

And this approach will work. I know this, because I've used it for the entirety of my professional career, sharing and fine-tuning this message for the past quarter century.

But be forewarned. This is not pop psychology. If you're looking for or expecting transcendental techniques cloaked in some mystic parable, you're going to be sorely disappointed. What you're holding in your hands is a solid, commonsense leadership strategy extracted from real-world situations and experiences. And I have absolutely no desire to keep any of it a secret from you.

Ground Rules

Baseball is an interesting sport. Like other internationally recognized sports, such as basketball, football, soccer, and rugby, it's governed by a predetermined set of rules. These official rules of the game are standardized, authorized, and well communicated. They're universally accepted and apply whenever and wherever people play the game of baseball—at home, on a visitor's field, or even at some neutral site.

But baseball is also unique. Besides playing within the established confines of the game's officially recognized rules, people also play baseball according to local ground rules. These are special rules particular to each ballpark or grounds. Unlike almost every other sport, baseball's playing field includes both fair *and* foul territory. To make things even more interesting, spectators line the playing field, frequently interacting directly with the players during the game. It's imperative that those participating define the ground rules in anticipation of situations in which obstacles in the field of play may interact or interfere with the ball in play or the players involved.

What does all this have to do with learning leadership? you might be wondering.

The answer is—everything.

Consider the thousands of officially recorded rules and regulations identifying both acceptable and unacceptable behavior of managers and supervisors. These apply to issues ranging from minimum wages, to taxation, to health and safety, to the environment, to governmental reporting, to discrimination, and so on. Most managers and supervisors know and document these rules and receive not only available but also often mandatory training relative to them. We'll refer to these as the official rules of the game.

Now consider the issue of leadership—specifically leadership in action. Managers and supervisors must know the official rules of the game, but they must also be able to lead as the game unfolds around them. They have to do their jobs while things are going well (in fair territory) and when things are going wrong (in foul territory). They must lead with the full knowledge that spectators (superiors, peers, subordinates, customers, clients, and stockholders) are not only watching the proceedings but will occasionally step in, interfering with the action, while play is still in progress. To succeed under such circumstances, the most effective leaders must recognize, master, and apply the ground rules that support proactive leadership.

Most games, including baseball, seem fairly basic when we view them from a one-dimensional perspective—on television, for example. However, the game becomes infinitely more challenging when one steps onto the field of play as a participant. The speed, competitiveness, expectations, pressure, and subtle nuances that affect the game's outcome all become readily apparent to the engaged participant.

That's how it is with leadership, too. Leadership may seem fairly easy to accomplish when discussed casually over a cup of coffee or when explored page by page, in a book like this one. But once you step onto the field of play—for example, the office, the plant floor, the mine site, the classroom—the game changes immediately. The objectives, deadlines, traditions, culture, and personalities all become critical elements that you must consider and include in the leadership equation.

This book explores 11 common sense, universal leadership ground rules that *Leaders Ought to Know* if their ultimate goal is to lead others with purpose, confidence, and effectiveness. These ground rules have been assembled from multiple sources (e.g., books, articles, workshops, training classes, observations, conversations, experiments, successes, and mistakes) over the past 30 years. They've been vetted for value and trustworthiness in the trenches over the same period. I share these ground rules with ultimate confidence that they will work for any leader committed to doing the same—making them work.

If you're ready, let's get started.

Chapter 1

Choosing to Lead

Ground Rule #1

All leaders are born, but none are born leaders;
Leadership is a choice, reinforced by individual effort.

Born Leaders—The Myth

Okay, I've got to admit it: I'm encouraged. I'm encouraged because it appears that you are genuinely interested in leadership, either for yourself or for others. By now, you've seen the cover of this book and have possibly scanned the table of contents—and you're still here. That's a good sign—because people without a genuine interest in leadership (and sadly there are many, though for the life of me, I cannot understand why) simply wouldn't have gotten to this paragraph. They likely would have bypassed this title completely, opting instead for some riveting work of fiction—dealing with vampires, illicit love affairs, or some complicated plot surrounding international espionage.

But, as we know, leadership isn't fiction. Leadership is real—real life, real time, and real important.

Oh, and thankfully—leadership can be *learned.*

I recently had a rather animated conversation with an individual who, for some misguided reason, didn't share my belief that leaders are not born but *made.* He tried repeatedly (and unsuccessfully) to convince me that a leader either has it or doesn't have it from birth—though I was never quite able to get this gentleman to specifically define what the *it* is.

I find his assertion to be very troubling—and here's why. If this man is right (and I don't for a moment believe he is), then there would be no reason to read this or any other book that deals with the topics of leadership, motivation, communication, problem solving, team building, or a litany of other subjects about people interacting with other people. Books— in addition to training sessions, coaching, mentoring, even personal life experiences—would be of no benefit and a total waste of time for those unfortunate souls born without the leadership *it.* Why? Because those who have *it* simply don't need this book, leadership instruction, or anything else; they've already got *it.* And those who don't will never be able to get *it*—try as they might—from this or any other book or educational effort. Now, to me, that's sad to even consider.

I'm more optimistic than that. I believe that every human birth brings with it the possibility of a new leader. A newborn child conceivably has the potential to learn and grow to become a famous leader in the mold of Abraham Lincoln, Mahatma Gandhi, Martin Luther King, or Mother Theresa. Or maybe the child will simply grow into a more common, albeit less publicly visible leadership role in his or her company, community, or family. But every single one of them can learn to lead, as can the rest of us.

How can I be so sure? Well, for one thing, I've witnessed the birth and development of three leaders firsthand: my children, who are no longer children but contributing adults who serve admirably in various leadership roles at their jobs, in their communities, to their peer groups, and in their homes. They are leaders not because I say they are, but rather because individuals have chosen, voluntarily and repeatedly, to follow them.

But they haven't always been leaders. I was physically present, an excited eyewitness, when each of my children entered this world. I watched with anticipation and awe as each took his or her first breath. I remember them looking remarkably similar—little pink, naked bundles of leadership potential. But I can assure you that not one of them, during their moment of entry into this world, leapt to his or her feet in that delivery room shouting, "Follow me!"

They were bundles of joy and potential, with their own unique personalities embedded in their DNA. However, they still had to undergo the processes of learning, growing, trying, and failing—while hopefully developing valuable lessons along the way. They forged ahead, continuing to grow, trying and failing, and learning again and again. They've become the leaders they are today as a result of the information, encouragement, feedback, and correction they've received from countless people—all driven by the uniqueness of their personalities and their level of personal desire.

I also know for certain that individuals can learn to lead because I've watched countless numbers of them do so over the past quarter century, in and through leadership training and coaching sessions I myself have been privileged to lead. Thousands of these dedicated professionals initially saw and defined themselves only in terms of their supervisory or managerial responsibilities. But over time, they were able to learn and adopt new principles and then specific techniques that enabled and even propelled them into effective leadership roles.

Finally, I know regular people like you and me can actually learn to lead because I did so myself. I've been on a personal journey of leadership discovery for more than 30 years, all the while attempting to learn, grow, and perform ever more effectively as a leader. I'm certainly not where I ultimately *want* to be; after all, leadership development, like most good things in life, is a journey, not a destination. However, I'm far beyond where I *used* to be. And the satisfaction that comes with that revelation is invaluable and energizing.

Yes, individuals can learn to lead, but whether they're my kids or your kids, my employees or your employees, me or you, the one thing we must do to grow and develop as leaders is to all first decide that we actually *want to lead*. And we must wholeheartedly believe that the effort required in learning to lead will ultimately be worth it.

Your Most Important Professional Decision

If I asked you to name the single most important professional decision you've ever made, how would you answer? Could you answer? Most people can't, which I know because I've asked this of thousands of managers and supervisors in countless training sessions over the past 25 years. This question often results in blank stares, diverted eyes, and more than a little head scratching. If the silence becomes too uncomfortable, a few brave souls eventually speak up in an attempt to offer some sort of answer:

"Well, I guess it was a good thing that I got my engineering degree."

"I can say for sure that going to work for a big company has provided me a broad, diverse professional perspective."

"Personally, I've been fortunate in that my job has allowed me to make a lot of money."

Though each is a legitimate response in its own right, do any of them really rise to the level of being rated the *single most important* professional decision? I don't think so.

To be fair, this question is a difficult one. Think about it: Even if you've only been working for a few years, you've already made thousands of individual decisions—and this list continues to grow steadily with each additional year of professional service. In fact, you'll probably make dozens, if not hundreds, of decisions this week alone. Admittedly, when considered individually and in isolation from the others, the majority of these decisions may seem rather insignificant. For instance:

Decision: Do I need to return this client's call now, or can it wait until Monday?

Decision: Is this report complete enough, or should I support it with a chart listing appropriate data?

Decision: Should I continue reading this book, or do I already know enough about leadership to get by?

Alone and separated from the wide array of other decisions we may be making, these individual decisions often don't appear to be terribly earth-shattering. But their cumulative effect is quite different.

Those of us with children are quick to remind them that making good decisions leads to positive outcomes. Conversely, making bad decisions invariably leads to less than desirable outcomes. Our past experiences teach us that this is true—and we wouldn't intentionally mislead our children, would we? But do *we* ever take time to consider the long-term implications of our individual leadership decisions—the ones we make incidentally, one at a time, without much forethought or planning?

I like to think of it this way: Every choice we make represents a brick that we are placing in the structure that will eventually become known as our reputation. Making the occasional poor or uniformed decision probably won't have much of an effect on our reputation over the long haul. It's the equivalent of unwittingly laying a single cracked brick surrounded by hundreds of solid bricks in a building's foundation. The chances are good that the solid surrounding bricks will support and protect the building's integrity from the weakness of the one flawed brick.

But if one were to recklessly, irresponsibly, and knowingly lay one flawed brick after another into the foundation of a building, that building's integrity would eventually be jeopardized, especially when (not if) that building was inevitably exposed to some sort of stress.

Of course, not all decisions are minor ones. We all realize that some are far more significant than others, representing professional game changers—cornerstones, if you will, in my building analogy. If one were to lay a cracked *cornerstone* in a building, one designed to bear the entire building's weight, nothing could be sure or guaranteed. Such critical decisions—to leave one company for another; to accept a promotion or transfer; to align oneself with a highly qualified mentor; to lie, cheat, or steal to get ahead; to ignore the importance of personal leadership development—can change the course of future events forever. But how can you readily distinguish between one seemingly innocuous run-of-the-mill decision and one of those monumental life changers? As many of us know, they can sometimes look eerily similar.

If Japan Can, Why Can't We?

The year was 1980. There I sat, a young human resources professional, fresh out of college, tending to the routine business of the day, when my boss called.

"Phil, come on over to my office. There's something I'd like to discuss with you."

"Oh, great," I instinctively thought, an immediate sense of dread creeping over me. "I'll bet he's got something else for me to do."

Had someone asked me at that very moment, I'm sure I wouldn't have categorized these initial thoughts as being negative. After all, I liked my job. I was the personnel supervisor for a large American manufacturing company. And I liked my boss. Jerry had hired me for this, my first job out of college, and for that, I was truly grateful.

But I must admit, I wasn't thinking much about the future—mine or the company's. Rather, I was satisfied where I was and not terribly interested in considering where I might be able to go, what I might be able to do, and what it might take to get me there. Simply put, I was comfortable—in retrospect, too comfortable. And unfortunately, I've since discovered that personal comfort is a mind-set far too many of us embrace, far too often.

"What's up, Jerry?" I asked, as I took a seat across from my boss.

Jerry leaned back in his chair and looked at me. "Phil, I need for you to watch a television program tonight. It's a NBC documentary called *If Japan Can, Why Can't We?*"

I was quickly relieved to learn my homework assignment wouldn't require a lot of heavy lifting. Or so I thought at the time. There was no way I could've known then that the minor decision to simply watch a television program would ultimately compel me to make the single most important business decision of my life.

That night, I watched the documentary, which prominently featured the work of an American statistician named W. Edwards Deming. I learned that the Japanese revered Deming for introducing statistical methods and systems, including statistical process controls (SPC), as critical steps in allowing that country's companies to regain their global stature as an innovative, quality-driven economic power following World War II. In the months and years after initially viewing the film, I continued learning more and became increasingly impressed with Deming's message. Beginning that night and continuing for years afterward, I studied Deming and his systems—not just his quality systems, but his systematic approach to management and leadership as well.

In his 1986 book, *Out of the Crisis* (Massachusetts Institute of Technology, Center for Advanced Engineering Studies), Deming wrote:

> *Long-term commitment to new learning and new philosophy is required of any management that seeks transformation. The timid and the fainthearted, and the people that expect quick results, are doomed to disappointment.*

Deming's transformational message and the commonsense warning it contained resonated with me as a young supervisor, aspiring manager, and fledgling leader. I discovered rather quickly that I was unafraid of "new learning and new philosophy," primarily because I was not yet entrenched in any particular *old* learning or *old* philosophy. My initial corporate experiences, such as working with supervisors and managers who were more than twice my age, prompted me to question the entrenched management philosophies of the day. Though I didn't recognize it at the time, I was in the midst of my own professional transformation. I was beginning to realize that a real need existed in most organizations for more informed, enlightened, impactful leaders, versus the traditional dictatorial, heavy-handed, top-down supervision or management style more prevalent at the time.

So way back then, a flickering image on a television screen led me to make a life-changing decision. I consciously and intentionally decided that I didn't want to just learn to be a *supervisor* or *manager*. Instead, I wanted to be transformed into a *leader* who had the professional responsibility to supervise and manage others. I also knew that I didn't want this transformation to be bound by the clock or the calendar. Since my entire career was ahead of me, I decided to do whatever it took, for as long as it took, to make this transformation a reality. Deming warned that expecting quick results would yield disappointment. Therefore, I settled in for the long haul, determined to learn and to practice what I was learning, every day going forward. And so I have.

That singular decision—to learn to be a *leader,* not a *manager*—has proven to be my most important professional decision—certainly more important than deciding which companies to work for or even to start and more important than money I've earned or invested. It was more important than books I've read or written—including this one. It has been said, "When the student is ready, the teacher appears." Apparently, I was ready when Deming appeared in my life. Though I never met him personally, Deming was my leadership system evangelist and I was one of his many converts.

The results of my decision to actively and doggedly pursue personal leadership development have proven to be nothing short of amazing. I could literally talk for hours about the transformation that has occurred in my life due to my ability to practice the leadership techniques I was learning. The results I've experienced personally are nicely summarized in

Deming's *The New Economics: For Industry, Government, Education* (1993), in which he observed:

> *The individual, transformed, will perceive new meaning to his life, to events, to numbers, to interactions between people.*

How true! Deciding to take and set out on this journey has impacted virtually every decision, large and small, while transforming my entire life for the better. I make decisions with purpose and intent. I'm fully aware and accepting of the responsibilities I'm to bear in professional and personal relationships I develop. My deliberate pursuit of leadership and what *Leaders Ought to Know* has expanded, elevated, and enriched the opportunities, experiences, and relationships in my life.

And the same can be true for you. Leadership is not reserved for a few. It's available to many, though it's unfortunately true that far too few ultimately choose to pursue it. But for special individuals like you who wish to be more effective leaders in their industry, business, community, club, religious institution, school, or even family, I'm absolutely certain this book can help lead them—and you—there.

Congratulations, You've Been Promoted! Now What?

Let's face the facts. Though we've already established that leaders can learn to lead, most of us were never formally trained to be a leader. The majority of the managers and supervisors I know initially earned their opportunity to be in a position of leadership because they were smart, hardworking, and really good at what they did technically *before* being promoted there.

The engineer had a proven ability to analyze blueprints and schematics in the search for inaccuracies. The accountant was adept at interpreting the nuances of a balance sheet. The salesperson was masterful at prospecting, developing, and closing new business. The production worker was exceptional at overcoming unplanned, unanticipated obstacles to meet and exceed established production goals and standards. They were all good at what they did because that's what they had studied and been trained to do. After years of hands-on experience, their proven aptitude and performance capabilities had elevated them to an acknowledged level of competence and visibility within the organization, thus earning them a positive reputation for the good they had done.

Then one day, the boss called this peak performer into her office and announced she had good news. After much careful deliberation, this person was being promoted to supervision or management. They were being elevated overnight into what most would regard as a leadership position.

But did that automatically make her a leader in the eyes of those around her, especially those she had been tapped to supervise, manage, and lead? Of course not. And for far too many of us, that's where the trouble begins.

This individual had proven herself confident and capable in her ability to read blueprints, create an amazing spreadsheet, exceed sales quotas, or build the product safely and efficiently. However, she was far less confident in her ability to communicate group objectives effectively, lead her newly acquired team through a process of consensual decision making, confront problems and individuals head-on, or successfully accomplish the dozens of other daily critical responsibilities that leaders are expected to complete.

This was all completely new territory to her. She hadn't been trained for this. Add to the equation that the employees and individuals this newly minted leader had been tapped to lead were watching, evaluating, thinking, and often saying from Day One: "Someone in an important leadership position like hers just ought to know better."

That's why this book is in your hands now—because there are a number of really important things that *Leaders Ought to Know* that most of us have never had the opportunity to learn.

The Doctor Is in, and the Patient Is Waiting

Let's summarize to this point. Some people—okay, most people—are pitched into the leadership fray without really knowing what to expect or do. They were born with the potential to lead but have not yet learned the critical leadership principles needed to be successful. They've worked hard in their previous positions and are now flattered to be recognized for their efforts with a promotion—a promotion that undoubtedly includes additional leadership expectations. Of course, there are also individuals who actively search out leadership positions and responsibilities but do so before being adequately prepared to accept them. We've all seen such individuals. Some of these people are able to rise to these occasions over time, while others flounder.

During my live leadership training sessions over the years, I have occasionally used a fanciful, somewhat ridiculous scenario for illustrative purposes. Regardless of the industry I'm working in—be it financial services, mining, manufacturing, or some other—I single out two of the training participants at random, calling them by name for the benefit of other audience members. (Here I'll use the names Jack and Janet.) The exercise unfolds as follows.

Me speaking to the entire group:

"Folks, you're probably not aware of it, but we have an individual with us today who has a hidden dream. Jack, here, has always wanted to be a surgeon. Ever since he was a little boy, he has fantasized about being able to save lives and help people with desperate physical needs. You may not have known this about Jack because he's a relatively private person. But this has been Jack's dream nevertheless. Isn't that right, Jack?"

Though slightly suspicious, Jack good-naturedly plays along. Others in the room are usually snickering by now, possibly considering the far-fetched nature of such a possibility. I continue:

"Earlier today, Jack decided to finally act on his dream of becoming a surgeon. He drove down to the local medical center and proceeded to the surgical unit. Once there, Jack walked purposefully past the 'No Admittance: Authorized Medical Personnel Only' signs and made his way directly into the surgical prep room, where he came face-to-face with that famous surgeon, Dr. Van Hooser—me—who had just finished scrubbing up for a waiting surgical patient."

I identify myself as the famous surgeon to the laughter of the group, including Jack. Janet is enjoying the activity, along with the others, oblivious to the fact that she will soon be drawn into this unfolding scenario as an unwitting participant.

"'Who are you?' I ask, as Jack enters my operating room.

"'Jack,' he answers simply.

"'No, young man, you don't understand. I don't really care who you are. I want to know—who do you think you are barging into my operating room uninvited?'

"'I'm sorry, Dr. Van Hooser, sir,' Jack explains. 'I'm here because I've always wanted to be a surgeon. I know I can do it. I know I can be successful. All I need is a chance. I need someone—you—to give me a chance to prove myself.'

"'Have you ever been to med school?' I ask pointedly.

"'No, sir, but I want to be a surgeon.'

"'Have you ever taken any anatomy or physiology classes?

"'No, sir, but I really want to be a surgeon.'

"'Have you ever been in a real surgical situation, even observing an actual surgery in progress?'

"'No, sir, but I really want to be a surgeon and I'm willing to try.'"

I, assuming the role as Dr. Van Hooser, pause for the sake of effect before continuing.

"'Young man, don't ask me to explain why I'm about to do what I'm about to do. But for some reason, my gut is telling me that you might just make it as an acceptable surgeon one day. Therefore, this is what I want you to do right now. Here's my scalpel. Take it. Now, there's a patient prepped and waiting on the other side of this door. Her name is Janet.'"

25

Choosing to Lead

Janet's attention is immediately arrested. Laughter ensues as the audience begins to anticipate what happens next. Everyone is laughing now, except Janet.

"'I want you to go through that door and attempt to remove Janet's appendix. If she makes it through the surgery, we can discuss the possibility of sending you off to med school sometime in the future so you can actually learn what you should know to be a surgeon.'"

Laughter intensifies. Finally, turning my full attention now to Janet, I ask:

"'So, Janet, how are you feeling right about now?'

"'Not too good! I think I want another opinion,' says Janet (or something to that effect)."

The room is fully engulfed in laughter now, including Jack and Janet. Once the laughter dies down, I make the following learning points.

"Folks, I think we all agree that the scenario I've just created is ridiculous, regardless of the angle from which you might evaluate it. It's absurd to imagine, whether you are in Jack's shoes, Dr. Van Hooser's shoes, and especially if you're in Janet's shoes. Agreed?

The audience agrees.

"However, I'm here to tell you that as ridiculous as it may seem, similar situations happen virtually every day in organizations across America and around the world. On a daily basis, organizations entrust their future to genuinely dedicated individuals who sincerely want to do well but who have received no specialized training or preparation and have not an inkling as to how to effectively lead, influence, and impact people to accomplish organizational goals such as productivity, profitability, quality, and safety.

"We are giving untrained, unqualified individuals a scalpel, in the form of the power of the position, without training them how to use it, and then encouraging them to go do surgery on their departments and on their employees.

"At the very same time, the employees on the other side of the door are waiting—even longing—for qualified supervisors, managers, and leaders to emerge to help them with the challenges they're facing, challenges they will never be able to overcome alone. They're desperately searching for someone who knows how to lead and can do so effectively. They're looking for someone to follow."

Accepting the Challenge

I know the challenges of leadership transformation firsthand. I've lived them in the various stages of my own supervisory and managerial career. I've seen them up close and personal every day for the past 25 years, as I've worked with hundreds of organizations around the world to develop and strengthen their respective leadership bases. And while embracing this is not easy, it's not impossible.

That's why I wrote this book. My professional mission in life is to provide organizations with the appropriate concepts, tools, and inspiration needed to help transform great people into great leaders. At the same time, I value the opportunity to work with individual leaders—both aspiring and experienced—to offer practical techniques and tools for being ever more effective in their current and future leadership roles.

As I prepare to share the critical principles that I believe will encourage and empower every person who honestly desires to be a better leader, I'll share two additional thoughts that reemphasize my own—and this book's—underlying assertion: that the essence of leadership development begins with a choice that both organizations and individuals need to consciously make.

A *Fortune* magazine article a few years back entitled "Leader Machines" by Jeff Colvin (October 1, 2007), reminded organizations that heightened levels of internal leadership, preparedness, and performance can provide a true competitive advantage. Specifically, the author wrote:

> *Your competition can copy every advantage you've got—except one. That's why the best companies are realizing that no matter what business you're in, the real business is building leaders.* (Page 98)

Second, in Jim Collins's book *Great by Choice* (2011, HarperBusiness), Collins introduces a concept he refers to as "10X." To Collins, a "10Xer" represents a company that has become successful over time, performing at a level that far exceeds others that might rightfully be considered contemporaries. I think Collins's 10X description describes aptly what I believe about peak leadership performers as well, especially when he writes:

> *They're not more creative. They're not more visionary. They're not more charismatic. They're not more*

ambitious. They're not more blessed by luck. They're
not more risk seeking. They're not more heroic.
They're not more prone to making big, bold moves.
[10Xers] . . . reject the idea that forces outside their
control or chance events will determine their results; they
accept full responsibility for their own fate.

And that is what I challenge you do: decide right now to take full responsibility for your own leadership fate. Don't leave your personal leadership development to chance or to the discretion of others. Remember, everyone can learn to lead if they will just decide to do so—but first, you must decide.

I would like to offer one more admonition before moving forward. Before you turn the page and begin reading, studying, and applying the principles that follow, *decide* that you will learn to be a leader and that, as a leader, you will *make a difference,* beginning today. Do it! Decide right now, right here, by making a personal commitment. Walk to a mirror, look at your own image, and say it out loud, "Beginning right now, I will do everything in my power to learn to be a better, more effective leader."

The decision you make today—right now—may very well prove to be the best professional decision you will ever make. It may be the key that unlocks the leadership transformation within you.

Chapter 2

Offer Service, Take Action

Ground Rule #2

Leadership is not position;

Leadership is the ability to offer service and the willingness to take action.

Management 101

I took my first business class, Management 101, as a college freshman in 1975. At the time, I admittedly didn't know anything about business, management, or much else of any depth or significance. But I did know one thing for sure: I had to pass Management 101 to eventually secure a business degree and to get on with my career.

Within the first 15 minutes of that first entry-level management class, our professor introduced us to what he called the four management functions. I remember the phrase distinctly. I wrote it down. He made a point of emphasizing those words. As a result, I felt certain they would reappear in some form as a future test question.

I was right. The four management functions did appear again—and not just once. They kept appearing and reappearing, again and again and again, in various tests, projects, studies, and discussions for the full four years of my business education. By the time I graduated from the university, business degree in hand, I was honestly pretty sick of hearing about these four functions and their various iterations. I was ready to move on—to cast off management *theory* and to embrace management *practice*.

But even then, I couldn't get away from the four management functions. Within hours of starting my first job out of college, I was surrounded by their reality yet again. And guess what? I still am. Though much has changed (and continues to change) since my college days, there's been one constant throughout my professional career: the continuing need to consider, evaluate, and embrace those four pesky functions. In fact, I fully expect those management functions to continue to impact the rest of my career—and yours.

The Four Management Functions

Whether you study the discipline of management at Harvard University, Oxford University, Murray State University (my alma mater), or any other highly acclaimed educational institution, the four management functions must be introduced and explored. This is because they serve as foundational cornerstones on which the structure of all management activity is built, supported, and maintained.

It's possible that you're a bit perturbed by now, since I've made several veiled references to these four management functions without explaining specifically what they are. I'll remedy that now. Simply put, the four management functions are the ability (and professional obligation) to effectively:

- Plan
- Organize
- Direct
- Control

These four verbs, each active by their nature, can seem incredibly simple and unremarkable to the uninformed, untrained, or inexperienced. But the opportunity for phenomenal success—or the threat of horrendous failure—precariously rests with them. Success or failure is ultimately dependent on how individuals and organizations apply these management functions in practice.

Volumes of business books exploring in depth these four functions' various applications have appeared over time. Still more have dissected the mistakes business managers have made in overlooking or underplaying the importance of one or more of them. As for this book, and for me, I have no such intent. My singular purpose is to explore the function of leadership and how it interacts (or differs) from the various functions of management.

The Four Resources to Be Managed

From Day One of my formal management education, my professors stressed the ultimate responsibility of managers everywhere is to plan, organize, direct, and control specific *resources*. I learned those resources generally represent four broad categories:

1. Physical (e.g., facilities, equipment, tooling, materials, and supplies, even natural resources)
2. Financial (e.g., labor performance, receivables/pay-ables, waste/scrap/shrinkage, time, and investments)
3. Technological (e.g., hardware/software, telecommunications, distance learning, electronic data management)
4. Human (e.g., employees, staff, labor)

The first three categories (physical, financial, and technological) are certainly a challenge to manage in their own right. However, when contrasted against the fourth category of human resources, even experienced managers will testify that the first three constitute a walk in the park.

If Not People, Who Then?

I was a member of a cross-functional production planning team early in my management career. My fellow managers and I had been sequestered for several days, working diligently to "plan, organize, direct, and control" the new product line's introduction. It was tedious but energizing work, as these new products presented significant potential opportunity.

After spending hours on dry, complicated issues like raw material sourcing, physical plant realignment, and project budgeting, I was excited when the time came to discuss how we planned to staff this new operation. I was excited because I know that people ultimately make the difference in any worthwhile undertaking.

The team leader announced, "Well, folks, we need to turn our attention to the people end of this equation."

We all heard a long, anguished sigh from the far end of the table. Heads turned in the direction of the production manager, who sat slumped forward in his chair, his eyes buried in the palms of his hands.

"What's wrong, Henry?" the team leader asked.

The manager slowly looked up, his head shaking slightly.

"I've enjoyed this project until now. It's been fun. But I've got to admit, this is the part of my job I hate the most," he replied, pausing briefly before adding, "My job wouldn't be bad at all if I didn't have to worry about people."

This man was a manager. Yet, by his own admission, the thing he hated most about his job was dealing with people. Such an attitude does not bode well for future leadership success.

Though it's one of the more memorable, that occasion is far from the only instance when I've heard supervisors and managers grouse about their interactions with people. Many managers readily accept the responsibilities that come with managing the physical, financial, and/or technological aspects of their jobs, primarily because they're able to maintain total control. But it can be a very different story when it comes to *managing* people. Unlike the other three resource groups, the human resource can—and will—think for themselves, ultimately choosing their own course of action, a course that sometimes proves to be contrary to a supervisor's or manager's desires.

The Six Management Objectives

The management plot thickens considerably when one considers the fact that coupled with one or more of the required resources, each management function must also be managed within the framework of ever-evolving business objectives, including:

- Safety

- Productivity

- Profitability

- Quality

- Innovation

- Engagement

The responsibility of managing these inherently complicated variables is not for the fainthearted; it is hard, important work. But hard as it may be, one truth must remain imminently clear: The physical, financial, and technological resources are, at the end of the day, still just *things*. Granted, they are critical, complex, valuable things—but things nonetheless.

But human resources are our people. If and when led appropriately, people are ultimately amazing creatures capable of amazing accomplishments. As nineteenth-century industrialist Andrew Carnegie put it: "Take away my people and leave my factories and soon grass will grow on the factory floors.

But take away my factories and leave my people and soon we will build bigger and better factories."

It's true, and always has been. People make the difference.

"What Do You Think?"

Whether we find ourselves building automobiles, mining natural resources, overseeing a hospital ward, or completing any of literally hundreds of other professional responsibilities managers and supervisors oversee daily, we're still expected to do our jobs safely, productively, profitably, with an unwavering commitment to quality. Few would argue these four.

But the last two items on the list—innovation and engagement—can be even more difficult. Innovation is founded on introducing and trying new ideas, processes, and techniques—a seemingly intriguing endeavor. Yet some people are less amenable to trying new things when it requires them to abandon old ideas, processes, and techniques, especially those they personally had a hand in developing.

Engagement, on the other hand, requires the inclusion and active participation of subordinates at a level beyond that commonly expected of them. I learned firsthand how crucial and challenging active employee engagement is when I was employed as a human resources manager in a large manufacturing environment. A production operation malfunctioned one day, causing a key process to grind to a stop and creating a critical production bottleneck. Dozens of production employees were immediately idled, and thousands of dollars were being added to the cost of building the product with each passing hour. We knew that we had to correct this situation as quickly as possible. To that end, managers and technicians from every discipline within the plant were summoned to the problem machine—even me.

I say even me because, admittedly, I was the least mechanically adept member of our entire upper management team. Yet, there I was, standing with other managers and technicians, observing the goings-on and hoping to be helpful in some way. It was there I noticed someone else standing apart, slightly farther away from the finicky machine than me. I was surprised at who it was—the operator of the machine in question. I moved over to him.

"So, Andrew, what do you think?" I asked innocently.

Surprisingly, my simple question opened the floodgate. Andrew started sharing in-depth observations, thoughts, and opinions on the matter at hand. I soon had more information than I could digest.

"Well, I was afraid something like this might happen," he began. "It's been acting strange for the past couple of days. I wrote up a maintenance work order, but no one ever came to me to discuss the problem. But today it got worse. The machine started triple cycling about two hours ago. I noticed the problem and adjusted the hydraulic leveler by a quarter turn, which has usually corrected the cycling problem in the past. But when I did it this time, I noticed an unusual, very slight and subtle vibration. I became concerned about the calibration of the unit once the final quadrant cycled back, and I discovered it was off by 26/100ths. Of course, you know what *that* means," he said knowingly. Then he paused, awaiting my response.

Know what that means? Was he kidding? Not only did I not know what *that* meant; I didn't understand 90 percent of what he'd just said. But the one thing I was sure about was that *he* knew what he was talking about. And yet, there he stood, alone and isolated from the conversations nearby. This guy was literally on the outside looking in, and he shouldn't have been. He was the person with the most practical knowledge of the machine in question, and he hadn't even been invited into the discussion. The operator who ran the machine 8, 10, sometimes 12 hours a day—and who had done so for several years—had been relegated to the sidelines, feeling anything but engaged.

Although I couldn't do much, I did what I could. I stepped in and asked a couple of the managers to listen to what the operator had to say.

"What is it?" one of the managers asked the operator brusquely, his question directed to Andrew.

Much to my surprise, the operator, so talkative just a couple minutes earlier, now hesitated. I was confused about why his response was not forthcoming. What had happened?

Sometime later, after more reflection, it hit me. I finally understood the difference in the operator's response to me—his heightened level of engagement—versus that to my fellow manager. It was simple. I had asked what the operator thought and then actively listened to what he had to say, whereas my colleague hadn't. That's it. When my colleague instead *demanded* information, Andrew chose to withhold what he knew.

The information Andrew possessed may or may not have helped the situation—we'll never know, because he

Offer Service, Take Action

consciously chose to withhold that information. Remember, human resources—our people—do what physical, financial, and technological resources never can or will. They make independent choices.

Mario and Luigi

In the mid-1980s, Japanese electronics company Nintendo released a very popular, early-generation video game called *Super Mario Brothers*. For those who didn't get to experience this, it was quite simple—and fun. Players used a joystick to maneuver the game's main characters, two brothers named Mario and Luigi, through the Mushroom Kingdom in a quest to rescue Princess Toadstool. This game world had gold coins scattered about for Mario and Luigi to collect that provided them greater protection and heightened powers. Some of the coins were available in plain sight and easily obtainable; others were secreted away in hidden locations, waiting to be discovered.

My young son, Joe, absolutely loved the game and became a master of it over time. He took great pleasure in challenging dear old Dad to play, then proceeding to whip me soundly. The game appeared to come easy for him, but not for me. I spent most of my time trying to reason my way through the course, invariably falling victim to some obstacle I could not anticipate, deduce, or avoid. Joe, on the other hand, played the game loose, with a relaxed, free-flowing manner, confronting each obstacle as it appeared and ultimately proceeding further in the game than I did—with many more gold coins to show for his efforts.

One night, after my son had gone to bed, I sat down to the game alone. I had a plan. I would play it again and again, practicing until I had memorized its sequence, along with the various locations of the gold coins. I then planned to challenge my son with the intention of besting him in our next head-to-head contest.

Some would argue that such a plan was far from the loving, fatherly thing to do. I agree. I'm admitting that my competitive spirit had gotten the better of me. I was tired of losing. I wanted to win for a change. From that desire sprang the motivation to hunker down in a darkened living room and forfeit sleep while practicing a childish video game.

But my plan worked. Well into the wee hours of the morning, I began to gain the knowledge and confidence I was seeking. I felt ready. I could barely wait for morning to dawn.

"Joe, how about a game of *Super Mario Brothers?*" I asked before Joe even had breakfast.

"Sure, Dad," he responded with predictable enthusiasm. "That'd be great."

"I'll go first," I said, seizing the controls while leading my new best friend, Mario, on a grand adventure through the Mushroom Kingdom, all the while raking in gold coins at a rate previously unknown to me. Joe was visibly impressed.

"Wow, Dad, you've never gotten this far before!" he exclaimed over my shoulder. "You're doing great!"

My son seemed to gain genuine satisfaction from observing my improvement and newfound skills. He continued to encourage me at every turn. A better man than me might have felt at least a pang of guilt for wanting to beat a son who was so supportive. But I didn't take time for such thoughts. I was

41

Offer Service, Take Action

single-minded. I was on a noble quest to save the Princess. I had a game to win.

Eventually, as expected, my skill (or luck) ran out. I reached the end of what I had known and practiced, entering into areas of the game previously unknown to me. I fell victim to one of the game's unforeseen obstacles. Nevertheless, by the time I turned the controls over to Joe, I had progressed further and had amassed more gold coins than ever before. I was almost giddy at the thought of imminent victory.

Joe sat down and started his turn. As expected, he moved effortlessly through the game's early stages and challenges, gathering a few gold coins as he went. But for reasons I couldn't understand, Joe seemed to spend less time than normal in certain stages of the game. In fact, I watched as he intentionally bypassed some gold coins that were easily available in plain sight.

"Joe, what are you doing?" I fussed. "You could've gotten a few more coins back there."

"I know," was all he said as he moved forward on his silent quest.

I was still well ahead in the gold coin count when Joe came to an obstacle that I had found particularly difficult to master: a pit that Luigi needed to leap over in order to move on in the game. The maneuver was so difficult for me that I had spent the better part of an hour the previous night practicing the timing required to make the jump successfully. Therefore, I was shocked when Joe approached the pit and made absolutely no effort to jump it at all. Instead, he intentionally ran right over the edge, directly into the pit below. It was more than I could handle.

"Joe!" I exclaimed. "What do you think you're doing?"

I admit that although I wanted to beat my son, I didn't want him to *give* me the victory. Before Joe could respond, I watched Luigi tumble over the edge into the pit. But instead of the game being over, Luigi reappeared unexpectedly, on a previously unseen ledge below. From there, Joe masterfully led Luigi into a hidden cave filled with an overabundance of gold coins—more than I could've ever imagined existed.

I looked on in utter disbelief as Luigi stood, raking in the coins. It was then that Joe casually responded over his shoulder, "See, Dad? There's a whole new world down here."

That's how it is with management and leadership. You can study and prepare for management challenges in a classroom, in the comfort of your office, even in isolation and solitude online. You can learn about management functions and resources. You can even stay awake over the course of an entire evening, cramming to master a particular concept, approach—or video game. But no matter how prepared you think you are, there exists a "whole new world" awaiting you once you accept the challenge of leadership. It's a world less defined by linear methodology that you learn and practice in some predetermined sequence (like I had attempted to do with *Super Mario Brothers*). The world of leadership is free-flowing, governed by universal principles and the use of solid reasoning and good old-fashioned common sense. But guess what? When a leader finds those hidden caves full of coins—in that new, previously unexplored world—the personal and professional rewards can exceed even your wildest imagination.

Commonsense Leadership

Scientist, botanist, educator, and inventor George Washington Carver, renowned for the agricultural discoveries he made while studying the simple peanut, once said, "When you do a common thing in an uncommon way, you will command the attention of the world."

I think Dr. Carver was on to something. Following his lead, I'm offering a common sense definition of leadership that will serve as the cornerstone for the balance of this book. I've drawn this definition from countless conversations with respected leaders. It is supported and overlaid by feedback I've received from thousands of conscientious followers, each having shared what they respect and appreciate about their leaders. I've then whittled down that information to the following practical, common sense definition of leadership:

Leadership is not position. Leadership is the ability to offer service and the willingness to take action.

This commonsense definition addresses two primary concepts: service and action. I'll address both of them shortly. However, let's start by looking at the first part of the definition, because before you can clearly understand what leadership is, you must clearly understand what it is *not*. Leadership is not position, plain and simple.

Over the past 25 years, I've delivered more than 3,500 presentations and training sessions on a variety of leadership topics to audiences on six continents. These audiences have ranged in size from less than a dozen people all the way up to several thousand. They've included academicians, corporate managers, high-ranking politicians, acclaimed scientists, best-selling authors, international dignitaries, successful entrepreneurs, professional athletes—and on and on. Time and again, I've stood before my audiences, tremendously impressed by their knowledge, sophistication, vision, courage, commitment, and level of accomplishment. But I've never, ever been impressed by an individual's position title. In fact, I'll go so far as to say that I doubt that anyone has been (or will be) impressed by your position title—with the possible exceptions of your mother and yourself.

Let's be honest with ourselves: Don't we all occasionally get caught up in reading our own press clippings? You know how much time, effort, and sacrifice was required to get you where you are today, regardless of where that might be. I suppose it's only human nature to derive a certain amount of personal satisfaction by occasionally whipping out your business card and watching a stranger get his or her first good look at your lofty title. But you better enjoy that fleeting moment, because it certainly won't last. Ultimately, people don't care what your title is. What they really care about is what you can do for them with that title and the position it represents—how you can help them improve their current situation.

I'm certain that leadership is not position. It is instead determined by our ability to offer service and our willingness to take action on our followers' behalf. Let's consider service first.

The Ability to Offer Service

Several years ago, I wrote a book titled "*Willie's Way: 6 Secrets for Wooing, Wowing, and Winning Customers and Their*

Offer Service, Take Action

Loyalty." The book's title gives clear indication of its focus—customer service. In *Willie's Way,* I use a common definition of *service* that almost everyone knows and can recite: *Service is meeting and/or exceeding the customer's expectations.*

In other words, we have not really assisted our customers appropriately until we've somehow met their personal service expectations—try as we might to convince ourselves otherwise. And just how do we determine what those service expectations are? Really, it's as simple as asking, listening, and observing.

We can take that same definition, adjust it ever so slightly, and apply it back to the practice of leadership.

Leadership is meeting or exceeding the
follower's expectations.

The same principle applies. Like customers, our followers expect specific things from their leaders. As a leader, you may or may not know what those expectations are. You should, of course, but you may not. But whether you're aware of these expectations or not—they exist. If a service professional doesn't meet—or preferably, *exceed*—customers' expectations, then the customer generally has the option, maybe even the motivation, to go elsewhere in search of better service.

A similar situation exists between leaders and followers. Followers everywhere expect their leaders to exhibit certain behavior, performance, and attitudes. These expectations can and will vary from one follower to another, based on each individual's values, past experiences, and needs. Whether followers ever discuss or publicly voice those expectations doesn't change the fact that they exist. And like a customer, a follower has choices. If a leader is not meeting and/or exceeding the expectations created in his or her follower's mind, that follower has two primary options to choose from: (1) They can quit and leave, or (2) they can quit and stay.

After having conducted dozens of exit interviews in my former managerial roles, I've found that the vast majority of employees who voluntarily change positions (via shift changes, department changes, resignations) do so in an effort to escape a supervisor or manager who is underperforming according to that employee's expectations. Rather than ride out the emotional roller coaster on which their boss is taking them, they opt instead to take their ball and go play somewhere else—to another shift, group, department, or even organization. And as we know, such actions can be expensive and disruptive on many different levels within a company— especially when they occur repeatedly.

As bad as it is to have an employee choose to quit and leave, it's worse when an employee decides to quit and stay. Maybe this person doesn't have the freedom, opportunity, or confidence to move to another shift, department, or company. Their only option is to stick around and tough it out under a superior who doesn't meet their expectations. Such a scenario can result in any number of predictable problems associated with quality, productivity, safety, morale, team interactions— or a combination of any (or all!) of these.

The Willingness to Take Action

Many of the leadership training sessions I've led over the years have been for corporate clients. On a number of these occasions, I've been approached by some anonymous employee while working in the client's headquarters—that is, someone who isn't participating in my leadership classes. These brief encounters have taken place in break rooms, hallways, parking lots, even at urinals! And the conversations usually begin and end the same way.

"Excuse me, sir," says the unknown conversant.

"Yes?" I respond.

"Aren't you that guy they've brought in to do leadership training for the supervisors and managers?"

"Yes, that's me," I admit.

"Will you answer one simple question that's been on my mind?"

"I'll try. Go ahead."

"Can you explain to me why they've hired you to come in here and tell these supervisors and managers new things that they should start doing to work better with the employees? Why can't you just get them to do the things they already know they should be doing, but aren't?"

Would you really like to know what's on your employees' minds? Well, right there's a good place to start. They're wondering why you don't do the things you already know to be important but never bother to act on.

Here's the lowdown on leadership from an employee's perspective. Followers want to see their leaders making an effort—doing *something!* The people with whom we come into contact don't expect us to say and do the *perfect* things. People are human; everyone makes mistakes, and our followers can accept that reality. What they can't understand, won't accept, and shouldn't have to expect is inattention, complacency, and inactivity.

I often ask my leadership audiences a simple question: "How many of you can think of at least one thing you know you need to do—something that would *definitely* make you a better leader if you did it?"

Usually, 100 percent of the hands in the room go up. Then I follow with this question: "Then what's keeping you from doing that thing?"

The responses I get next have become predictable over time.

"I would do it if I knew how."

"I would do it if I had time."

"I would do it if I thought it mattered."

This book is specifically designed to share many of the hows of leadership performance. But, I won't mislead you. It *does* take time—both to read the book and to apply and master the essential principles contained here. Remember, there are no shortcuts in the journey to becoming an effective leader. You must choose to pay attention. You must choose to avoid complacency. It does matter! But it's up to you to choose to *take action.*

Chapter 3

The Essential Element

Ground Rule #3

Leaders cannot function in a vacuum;

Leadership requires willing and able followers.

The Essential Element

It should be clear to you by now that leadership is not a spectator sport. You can't sit passively on the sidelines, expecting the desirable objectives of leadership growth, influence, and impact to mysteriously manifest themselves in you, because it's not going to happen. To be effective as a leader, you must get in the game. You must *engage*.

As discussed in Chapter 2, effective leaders must be willing to offer desired service and be able to take appropriate action. However, it's fair to assume that you may have some questions at this point, questions like, "Yeah, Phil, but where do I start?" "Who exactly should I be serving?" and perhaps the most pressing question, "What should I do first?"

Personally, I've always believed the best point from which to begin any worthwhile, long-term undertaking is to invest the necessary time up front to identify whatever that thing's essential element is. That is, determine the make-or-break aspect of the deal.

Let's assume you're in the market for an automobile. You're admittedly flexible when it comes to considering what you want; you're open to either a new or preowned model, a coupe or a sedan, a red or blue paint scheme. But the one nonnegotiable in your personal decision making is that your next vehicle must have an automatic transmission. If various automobiles you look at have every other option you could conceivably desire but are available only with a straight shift, you already know there will be no deal. An automatic transmission is the essential element.

Or suppose you're in the market for a new house. You may be open to a ranch style or a Cape Cod, a small lawn or a large lot with trees, a house on a neighborhood cul-de-sac or one farther out in the country. However, the one thing for certain is that the next house you buy must be located in a predetermined school district. If it's not, you may have your choice from the residential equivalents of the Taj Mahal, but it makes no difference; you're not moving. The school district is the essential element.

So it is with your leadership journey. You must know what the essential element of leadership is *before* you seriously begin the work necessary to identify opportunities, solidify your actions, and ultimately, build your leadership foundation. If you are at all unclear regarding the essential element of leadership, then confusion, distractions, and missed opportunities are sure to follow.

Leadership Begins and Ends with Followers

A few years ago, I was discussing this very point with a group of corporate managers during a leadership training session. I had posed the question, "What is the essential element of leadership?" A spirited discussion ensued.

"Of course, the essential element of leadership is vision," one opined. "Without vision, how would anyone on a team be able to distinguish the long-term goals and objectives?"

"I agree that vision is important," offered another, "but, if a leader lacks charisma or isn't able to connect with those he or she is attempting to lead, nothing of any real consequence is ever going to happen."

"Well, as important as vision and charisma are, I think they both pale in comparison to respect," offered still another. "The only way to be effective as a leader is to earn the respect of the people who report to you. Otherwise, no one is going to follow you anywhere. Respect must be the essential element of leadership."

And so the conversation continued. I played ringmaster during this "I think this; yeah, but what about that?" portion of the program. I wasn't offering my own viewpoint, but instead focused on facilitating the discussion and encouraging everyone with an opinion to jump into the fray. Every perspective, different as it may have been from the one before, initially appeared plausible; they were well-thought-out and effectively

The Essential Element

communicated. Each person seemed ready to support their individual choice with firsthand testimony—a personal story—as to why he or she thought their idea of what a leader must have was the most important quality. Eventually, as the discussion began to wane, the time came for me to share my perspective.

"Great discussion!" I admitted. "If nothing else, we've already learned that it's best to evaluate practical leadership from a variety of vantage points. And from my point of view, you're all right to suggest that leaders benefit from being well versed and capable of communicating a clear vision, with a high level of enthusiasm in a charismatic way, all the while utilizing the respect that they've earned over time. But honestly, I think you're all wrong if these are the answers you're offering to my original question. Your answers imply that the essential element has eluded each of you."

The group was paying close attention now. I suspect they were mentally preparing their rebuttals, anticipating some sort of need to defend their initial answers.

I continued: "Let's take a slightly different approach to see if we can come to an agreement regarding the essential element of leadership. Instead of using the word *essential,* what if I asked instead, 'What is the single element without which you, me, or *anyone* could ever lead?'"

Silence temporarily fell over the room as the group considered the new question. People sat mute, carefully mulling their next response. Finally, a solitary voice arose from the middle of the pack.

"Would it be followers?" a young woman asked timidly, almost apologetically.

Immediately, people started to agree. A few smiled, some snickered, as the majority of the group nodded in agreement.

"Ladies and gentlemen, we have a winner!" I announced. "The one thing the very best leaders among us never forget is that when all the veneer and noise surrounding the various philosophical concepts of leadership are stripped away, it's still people who remain at the very heart of leadership."

People to lead—who, from this point forward, I'll refer to as *followers*—are the key. No leader anywhere, anytime, can lead anything without active participation from willing and able followers. Therefore, as important as many other factors are in rounding out the performance of a good leader, we must never forget that followers have been, are, and will always be the *essential element* of leadership.

When I consider the need for people in the leadership equation, my mind often drifts back to a cartoon I received from a program participant several years ago. The cartoon's single frame depicted a solitary figure, disheveled and laboring mightily. Beneath the picture, the caption read: "There they go down the road and I must run and catch them—for I am their leader!"

Humorous as the cartoon and its sentiment may be, its message hits uncomfortably close to home for far too many of us. Though we fancy ourselves to be high-performing leaders, the reality is that we succeed only through the consistent, concerted efforts of dedicated followers—individuals who are willing, able, and available to follow our lead.

Three Primary Assumptions

My practical leadership experience has taught me that three primary assumptions deserve careful consideration when determining why a follower might or might not choose to follow you.

Assumption #1: There is a dire need for strong, effective leadership in every aspect of work and life.

Do you agree? Think about virtually any arena of life—politics, education, business, religion, relationships, the family. Each is affected directly and significantly by the quality (or lack thereof) of leadership available. Followers inevitably grow or falter, benefit or suffer, as a direct result of the quality of the leadership they experience.

A good leadership example paves the way for followers to maximize potential, in pursuit of personal and organizational goals and objectives. The absence of a good leadership example—or worse still, the presence of *poor* leadership—can cause followers to hesitate, stagnate, or even regress over time. That's why a struggling sports franchise chooses to fire the coach or general manager and not the players when things are not progressing in a positive manner. Without a visible example of positive, proactive, engaged leaders, his followers are bound to suffer mightily when they don't have a good model from which to learn and to emulate.

Assumption #2: People desire to be led.

Do you personally know more followers or leaders? Most people I talk with know more followers. And when you think about why that might be, the answer is actually pretty easy to discern. There are significantly more followers than leaders in the world today because most people conclude it's easier to follow than to lead.

Leadership requires personal visibility, sustained effort, and making difficult decisions. Leadership requires personal commitment. Leadership requires observable and measurable results and the ability to personally assume critical responsibilities.

When we consider all these kinds of requirements, is it any real surprise that most people recoil and shy away from what they see as the burden of leadership? It's a simple cost/value proposition for most, and many feel that the up-front costs—the personal sacrifices—are simply too great to endure with no guaranteed payback in the end. And while only a minority will make those sacrifices, they do so with the faith that it will allow them to help others—which will ultimately prove to be worth the effort.

On the heels of this question about knowing more followers or leaders, here's another important one to consider: Why would a person—any person—voluntarily choose to follow and support someone else?

I've posed this question to groups representing various cultures and ethnic backgrounds around the world. I've found the primary answers to be virtually the same, regardless of which of the Earth's continents the respondents may hail from. I've received many legitimate responses over the years, but three in particular surface repeatedly: People voluntarily choose to follow and support another person because (1) they like them, (2) they respect them, and (3) they trust them.

All three of these answers are warm, fuzzy, and fairly predictable. Oh, did I mention that all three are also wrong? Unfortunately, they are. If you're not convinced, let me prove it to you by providing a healthy dose of common sense and ask you to honestly consider your answers to these three questions:

1. Have you ever voluntarily followed and supported someone you did not like? (Yes or No)

2. Have you ever voluntarily followed and supported someone you did not respect? (Yes or No)

3. Have you ever voluntarily followed and supported someone you did not trust? (Yes or No)

If you answered yes to any or all of these three questions, you've proven my point. There are always going to be situations when we find ourselves in a place where we *have* to follow people we may not necessarily like, respect, or trust. But why would we do that?

We do it for one fundamental reason. Simply put, *we need their help.* It's always nice (and definitely more comfortable) to follow and support people we like, respect, and trust. But despite personal misgivings, we will also follow people we don't like, don't respect, and don't trust if they appear willing and able to secure for us something we want or need—things we can't figure out how to do or secure for ourselves.

Take a minute to reread the last few paragraphs. When you do so, you may notice a fair amount of leadership and motivational theory. But you'll notice, as you read further, that this theory is encased in the commonsense reality of human behavior. People desire to be led because they want or expect their leaders to help them get, do, or be what they either cannot or will not get, do, or be for themselves. Most people prefer following others to wrestling with the difficult job of making critical decisions and taking decisive actions alone, with no guarantee of success and no one to lean on (or blame) if those actions prove unsuccessful.

It's true. People—almost all of us—at some level, desire to be led.

Assumption #3: Leaders can make a difference that will last beyond their time.

This is the most important assumption, as far as I'm concerned. It's the very reason I've dedicated my time and effort over the past 30 years to the formidable tasks of learning and applying leadership to my own personal and professional situation—*and* conscientiously helping other people do the same. The fact is, I want to make a lasting difference. And I want you to make one, too.

Think about it this way. My father died suddenly of a heart attack less than two months past his 60th birthday. He was smart and talented. Though he lacked much formal education, he possessed considerable knowledge and life skills in critical areas such as understanding human behavior, proactive negotiations, and the value of a work ethic. I and my siblings were certainly positively affected by his modeled life example.

But as capable as he was, my father never took any great personal interest in developing or practicing his formal leadership skills, though the potential to do so was as available to him as it is to all of us. In fact, on more than one occasion, he resisted opportunities to assume leadership roles within organizations important to him. He preferred to follow rather than lead in those environments.

Please understand: There was nothing inherently wrong with his decision to be a follower. It did not make him or the work he did weak or ineffective. However, every decision comes with accompanying consequences. The consequences of my father's decisions showed themselves down the road in terms of the limited opportunities he had to make a lasting difference beyond his immediate sphere of influence (our family, his immediate friends).

I chose a different path. I determined early on in my career that I wanted to learn everything possible to make myself a better leader. In turn, I've always wanted to help others interested in doing the same—people like you. As we share what we know with others, our sphere of influence predictably expands and reaches into areas—and lives—we could've never otherwise imagined. Our words, actions, and behaviors have the opportunity to live on through our leadership influence—even beyond our time on Earth in the words, actions, and behaviors of others we have affected.

The Leadership Lie

Since my commitment is to continuously work to make myself a better leader (while helping you do the same), I feel a moral obligation to sound a cautionary note here. The scenario I'm about to describe can begin innocently enough but can transform itself over time into a rather insidious development. Thus, this word to the wise: Beware the leadership lie.

In Chapter 1, I mentioned that many people get their first taste of professional leadership when elevated to the role of supervisor or manager. That can be a heady time for many of us. We're justifiably proud that our efforts, dedication, and accomplishments have been publicly acknowledged and rewarded through promotion.

Yet, it can also be an uncertain time. Despite the public recognition and acclaim, there often exists, way down deep, a nagging concern, a question as to whether you can actually perform as admirably at the next level as you did at the previous one. You're firmly committed to future success, but you recognize that you have much to learn. Such periods of personal uncertainty can lead to insecurity and vulnerability. And when personal doubt is left to fester like that, it can provide fertile soil in which this particular leadership lie can take root and grow. But remember, it begins innocently. Here's how.

Your recent promotion is now public knowledge. You're receiving congratulations and good wishes from a variety of individuals as you prepare to assume your new job's practical responsibilities.

"Beverly, I'm glad I caught you," the well-wisher begins. "Congratulations on your recent promotion."

It's important to point out here that this well-wisher is quite possibly a highly respected individual within the organization. It's possible, even probable, that you've known him for an extended period. And not only do you know him, you genuinely like, respect, and trust him, and you have every reason to believe the feeling is mutual. There has never been any bad blood between you, and there have been ample indications that this person wants nothing but the best for you and your career. These are the exact reasons that this particular lie can be incredibly dangerous when a trusted individual delivers it. It comes to us with no flashing warning signs.

"I'm so proud of you," this well-wisher continues. "I can't think of a more deserving person for that supervisory position. I'll tell you right now, I'm predicting great things for you in the future. And to help in that regard, even though you haven't asked for it, I'm going to offer you an important piece of advice. I strongly suggest you take it.

"Here's my advice—don't get too close to your employees. Avoid this, because you're sure to find yourself needing to make a tough professional decision involving one or more of them at some point. If you've managed to keep your distance from them, you won't have to separate your personal feelings from your professional responsibilities. I think you'll find that it's just a whole lot easier to supervise or manage people if you don't get close to them to begin with."

There it is—the ultimate leadership lie, served up on a silver-tongued platter. As nonthreatening, even flattering as it may initially seem, it's still a lie—a falsehood, a fabrication, a misrepresentation, an untruth. Have you heard it yourself? I certainly have.

How Close Is Too Close?

Please notice that I haven't suggested this leadership lie is a *malicious* lie because, frankly, I don't believe it is. I sincerely trust that people doling out this advice aren't out to intentionally harm, derail, or destroy your ability to lead. In fact, this person was more than likely merely reciting something he himself had been told at some earlier point in his career. But a lie is still a lie—despite the intention. And if you act on this specific lie, it has the potential to do significant future damage to the leadership foundation you're establishing.

Let me offer a counterpoint to this well-wishing, advice giver. Whereas this person cautioned you not to get too close to employees because it's easier to supervise or manage people if you're not close to them, my advice is quite different. I say it this way: "You *can* be a supervisor or manager without getting close to your followers; however, you *cannot* be a leader *unless* you get close to your followers."

Remember the narrative from Chapter 2. Supervisors and managers supervise and manage *things*—physical, financial, and technological resources. Leaders, on the other hand, lead *people*. And the processes required to do each are remarkably different. To suggest that it's as easy to lead people as it is to manage some inanimate object or process is, at the least, wishful thinking and, at the most, plain old foolishness. People expect—and deserve—more from their leaders. Common sense tells us that people aren't likely to follow you if they know you've never taken the time or made the effort to get to know them personally. After all, if you haven't invested in them as your followers, why should they invest themselves in you as their leader?

· Now, when I suggest that a leader should get to know his or her followers, I'm *not* suggesting that you date them, go on vacation with them, or feel compelled to have them over to your house for cookouts on the weekends. Such activities may very well be far too personal and, as a result, professionally inappropriate.

However, I *am* suggesting that the act and art of becoming an engaged leader requires people to make the effort and

63

The Essential Element

investment necessary to get to know their followers—as well as their goals, talents, and aspirations. And it's just as important to know their fears, failings, and frustrations. Common sense again tells us that we cannot possibly lead effectively if we have little or no idea of what motivates, demotivates, compels, or demoralizes our followers.

Know Your Followers

In addition to the assertion that the essential element of leadership is followers, *Leaders Ought to Know* encourages leaders to do the very opposite of what this leadership lie suggests: make every effort to know more, not less, about those individuals we're interested in leading. Therefore, let's consider the practical reality of knowing your followers.

If you have children, have been around children, or have ever been a child, you know that every child is different. And because every child is different, the best way to connect with a child individually is to show interest in and get to know that child for who and what he or she is. That includes taking an interest in what is of interest to him or her. And as stated previously, it takes time and effort to get to know those things.

The very same thing is true with followers. It takes time and effort to get to know them. Once you make a genuine effort to get to know them as individuals, not just as somewhat anonymous, nondescript members of your work team, they will continue to feed you information about themselves as they become ever more comfortable with you and how you might use such information to help them.

But let's not get too far ahead of ourselves just yet.

When I'm working on-site with client organizations, I often challenge the supervisors and managers in my sessions by asking them specifically what they know about their employees, their followers. At first, most appear to be fairly confident, as if they know quite a lot. Of course, some do. But as I begin to ask specific questions, that confidence begins to melt away for many. For instance, I often ask how many of them know:

- The names of their followers' spouses or life partners?

- Where those spouses or partners work and what they do there?

- Specific details related to their followers' children—their ages, activities, and accomplishments?

- Their followers' birthday and service anniversary dates?

- Their hobbies and interests away from work?

As I indicated before, some of the best leaders are remarkably adept at gaining and using this knowledge. They know a lot about their followers. But unfortunately, even more aren't—and don't. Most of us know that we need to know more. Some of us are hard-pressed to explain *why* we don't know more. But the fact remains—we don't. And the not-so-obvious truth for leaders is that the less you know about your followers, the more likely they are to choose to follow someone else. Oh, they may continue to report to you. But if you don't know them and you're making no observable effort to correct that deficiency, there's a very good chance that they'll look to someone else for leadership.

The Essential Element

So what should leaders know about their followers? I have already indicated a few things; admittedly, some are easier than others. But all are important. And each thing that we should know has a definitive purpose. But let's start with first things first, shall we?

Who Are You?

Several years ago, I was leading an on-site leadership development workshop for a Florida law enforcement agency. We'd spent the morning discussing the practical value of leaders knowing their followers. We had talked extensively about the importance of developing knowledge of the backgrounds, talents, skills, and career aspirations of the people we wish to lead. During the morning break, one class member approached me.

"Sir," he began very officially. "Something's bothering me."

"I'm sorry to hear that," I said. "Is it something I can help with?"

"Yes, sir, it is," he said with a matter-of-fact tone. "You've taken quite a bit of time telling us a lot of important things we should know about our followers, but I think you've missed the single most important thing a leader ought to know."

There was a no-nonsense quality to his words, tone, and demeanor. He had my full attention.

"It's certainly possible that I've missed something critical. But you're going to have to help me out. What is it that you think I've missed?" I asked curiously.

"The name," he said bluntly.

"Excuse me?"

"The name," he repeated more emphatically, with slightly more emotion. "A leader's got to know his follower's name. It's imperative. If he doesn't know the person's name, all the rest of the stuff you've been talking about doesn't mean squat."

(Author's note: He didn't really say "squat." But on the off chance my mother reads this chapter, I didn't want to write what he really said.)

I fought back an involuntary chuckle. *Maybe this guy's playing with me*, I thought. *Surely he's joking.*

But he wasn't joking. He was serious, very serious. I gathered myself, realizing there was more I needed to know.

"Well, of course, knowing the names of those we wish to lead is important. But isn't that almost a given?" I asked.

"It wasn't for the jerk I work for," he said, before launching into the following story.

"I've always wanted to be a cop. After high school, most of my classmates headed off to college, to the military, or directly to work. But I enrolled in the police academy, because being a police officer was all I ever wanted to do. So I worked hard and graduated with honors several months later. Almost immediately, my hometown police department hired me as a patrol officer. They gave me a patrol car, a uniform, and a gun. Man, I was living the dream—my dream. I was finally a cop, with a job right where I grew up.

"I worked the streets as a patrol officer for five years. I don't mean to brag, but I must've done a pretty good job, because I was always getting some sort of letter of commendation from the mayor, the police chief, or other big shots in the department. But honestly, that didn't really matter all that much to me. I wasn't working for recognition. I was just trying to be the best cop I could be. I planned to be here for the long haul. I was gonna be one of those career guys.

"After about five years on patrol, I voluntarily transferred into the investigations unit. Nobody made me do that. I did it because I wanted to learn as much as possible about this entire profession. As an investigator, I took off my uniform and put on a suit. I climbed out of my patrol car and sat behind a desk. I came off the street and into police headquarters. I'd been working as an investigator for almost three years when it happened.

"I made a quick stop in the men's room at headquarters, but I was running late for an appointment. It was my fault. I admit it. I should've watched where I was going, but as I rushed out of the bathroom, I physically ran directly into the chief of police. That was embarrassing.

"'Excuse me,' I said, real polite to the chief. But he just stood there, glaring at me, all stern-faced. Finally, he spoke up.

"'Who are you?' he asked me coldly.

"'Officer John Doe, sir,' I said." (Actual name withheld to protect the innocent.)

"'What do you do?' he said.

"'I'm an investigator with the department, sir,' I said.

"'How long have you been here?' he said.

"'Almost eight years, sir,' I said.

"He didn't know anything about me—not even my name. I'd worked for the department for almost eight years, and even though he was a fellow cop, he didn't have a clue who I was. That was bad enough, but it got even worse. Do you know what he said next? He looked straight at me, almost like he was looking right through me, and then he said, 'I'm a busy man,

I don't have time for details.' That's all. He just said that, then he brushed right by me and left me standing there feeling like some sort of idiot.

"I'll tell you one thing, buddy. I'm not the only one that needs this training. If that jerk doesn't even know the names of the people who make him successful, well then, he needs this class worse than the rest of us."

Yes, and Then Some

I've had hundreds of conversations regarding various leadership issues over the years, but none is more vividly etched in my mind than the story that young police investigator shared with me that day. I have shared it with numerous audiences over the years. Predictably, people are incensed at the chief's level of insensitivity.

"That's terrible," various folks have said to me. "Why, he ought to leave."

Who ought to leave? The investigator or the chief? To my way of thinking, it certainly shouldn't be the investigator. This young professional had spent the better part of eight years honing his craft, doing his job to the very best of his ability. And while this police chief may have been a great administrator, overseeing significant resources, he failed miserably as a leader in one critical conversation with one of his subordinates—an indirect follower. As far as I'm concerned, if anyone needed to go, it ought to have been the chief—right?

Well, hold on now. Let's not rush too quickly to final judgment. In the spirit of fairness, haven't we all made mistakes? Haven't we all overreacted on one occasion or another?

Hasn't it been said by a leader far wiser than us, "Oh, ye without sin, let him cast the first stone?"

So for just a moment, instead of being a rock chucker, try to see yourself instead as a fence mender. Assume, if you will, that you're that police chief. And while you're at it, go ahead and admit that you made a mistake—an honest, shortsighted, callous mistake, not a malicious, ill-intentioned mistake. You just weren't thinking in that moment.

For the sake of argument, imagine yourself asking those three rather cold questions: Who are you? What do you do? How long have you been here? But instead of capping your blunder with that thoughtless statement, "I'm a busy man, I don't have time for details," let's consider another approach to reconciling your professional misstep with a professional recovery.

As the young man stands in front of you, shocked at your questions and at the full realization of just how little you know about him, what if you countered with something like this:

"John, first of all, I'm sorry. This is terribly embarrassing and totally uncalled for. There is no reason that I should not know who you are, what you do, and what your contributions to this department have been over the past eight years. I know it's a lot to ask, but I hope you can forgive my ignorance.

"Listen, do you have a few minutes now or maybe sometime real soon? I'd love to sit and talk with you and get to know you better. And maybe in the process you could give me some ideas on how to keep me from repeating this ridiculous, embarrassing episode with someone else in the future."

Would the outcome be any different? Would the young investigator go on his way with the same lingering animosity that bubbled to the surface during his recounting of the story? I don't think so. Sometimes, with a little effort and a little common sense, one can snatch victory (or at least reconciliation) from the jaws of defeat.

Remember—every leader will experience some measure of failure sooner or later. It's a predictable part of the leadership development process. But failure need not be fatal to our leadership aspirations. In fact, from the perspective of our followers, failure can be a good thing. Failure can make us appear more human and approachable—but if, and *only* if, we are willing to accept and admit our mistakes and use what we learn moving forward.

Chapter 4

A Recipe for Respect

Ground Rule #4

Leaders don't plan to be disrespected;

Leaders practice universal principles that earn respect.

WWYFS

The previous chapter focused on how critically important the *follower* is in the leadership equation. Since you're still reading, I trust that means you have accepted this premise—at least in theory. This is good news; now we can dive deeper into the complexities of the leader-follower relationship.

One of the best parts of leading training workshops is having the opportunity to interact with clients in their own workplace environments. The ornate trappings so often found in hotel or conference center meeting rooms are stripped away. As a result, I've found that on-site programs—conducted in familiar surroundings where real work is getting done—tend to have a more freeing, engaging effect on participants.

One group activity I enjoy introducing is an interactive exercise I call "What Would Your Followers Say?" Here's how the exercise normally unfolds.

The training room is filled with supervisory and managerial personnel from within the organization. These individuals may be high-ranking, 20-plus-year veterans or rank amateurs just wading into the sea of supervisory responsibility. My introductory comments would go something like this:

"We're here to explore leadership in a practical, nontheoretical way. Therefore, I'm about to pose a question. Once you have an answer in mind, jot it down. When all are ready, I will ask each of you to share your response. Here goes.

"I want you to think about the *best* leader you've ever known. Don't tell me or anyone else who that person is, but do keep your mind focused on that person. Once you're envisioning him or her, I want you to choose one word that best describes what made this leader so effective."

Without making any additional comments, I watch as program participants drift away in thought. Some begin writing almost immediately; others tend to smile faintly as they recollect some pleasant memory. After a few brief moments of silent contemplation, I speak up and begin selecting participants at random to share their chosen words of description.

"Randy, will you start us off? What word would you use to describe the best leader you've ever known?"

"Well, the person I have in mind was extremely fair," responds Randy.

I write the word fair *on a flip chart in the front of the room.*

"Thanks, Randy. Okay, what about you, Barbara?"

"My favorite leader was compassionate," she says.

Compassionate *goes up on the flip chart. And so goes the process. I query each participant until I've captured and displayed all descriptive words on the flip chart for the group. While working with hundreds of different clients over the years, I've taken great pains to compile a comprehensive list of the descriptive words collected during this particular exercise. I have amassed more than 300 of them.*

"Okay, folks, thanks for thinking and sharing regarding the best leader you've ever known. Now, take a minute to think about the *worst* leader you've ever known. What word would you use to best describe him or her?"

Spontaneous chuckles can usually be heard scattered around the room. Participants seem to relish this activity.

"Okay, who'd like to start?" I ask.

A voice calls from the back of the room. "I'll start, but first I want to make one thing clear: The guy I'm thinking about wasn't my leader. He was just somebody I had the misfortune of working for. I'd never follow somebody who acted like that dud." The man continues, "The guy was unbelievably selfish. Regardless of what was going on, it was all about him!"

With the ice broken, the floodgates open. Before I can finish writing selfish *on the flip chart, another person has jumped into the discussion to offer a less-than-admirable quality—then another, and another. By the time people finish sharing, an interesting collection of words have been compiled. Actual words (taken from the compiled list) like* selfish, spoiled, disorganized, liar, dictator, clueless, scatterbrained, incompetent, unprepared, *and* two-faced, *as well as several ultradescriptive R- and X-rated terms that I simply won't share here. (Sorry, I understand that inquiring minds want to know.*

A Recipe for Respect

But what would my granddaughter think about her granddad sharing such words?) Finally, after several minutes of collecting and considering descriptive words regarding the best and worst leaders, I wrap up the exercise.

"It's obviously pretty easy for us to remember our best and worst leaders. And we know that each of you could support every word you used to describe these leaders with accounts of actual experiences, stories, and circumstances that you remember vividly. Am I right?"

The group agrees. Then I continue.

"Though this has been fun, we haven't even asked the most important question yet, which is: What words are your followers using to describe *you* when they talk with colleagues, family, friends, and maybe even total strangers?"

That's right. Your followers have a special word they commonly use to describe you to others, too. And like it or not, in their minds, you have *earned* that word—whatever it may be, positive or negative—through your past words, deeds, or attitudes. Of course, if you aren't thrilled about the word they might use, you can always begin working now to change it via your future words, deeds, and attitudes. That's called being proactive. Being proactive is a necessary step toward earning the respect of others.

Respect Is as Respect Does

In 1995, the movie *Forrest Gump* (based on Winston Groom's novel by the same name) won Academy Awards for Best Picture, Best Director (Robert Zemeckis), Best Actor (Tom Hanks), Best Adapted Screenplay, Best Visual Effects, and Best

Film Editing. But the best and most memorable part of the movie for me was a line delivered by actress Sally Field, who played Forrest Gump's mother. Do you remember it, too? If so, repeat it now.

"Stupid is as stupid does."

It's true, isn't it? Regardless how intelligent, highly educated, or experienced we may be, followers are going to judge our level of leadership competence by what they *see us do*. And the same concept comes into play regarding the issue of respect and its impact on personal leadership.

If there is such a thing as a no-brainer in the discussion of leadership, it may be the universally accepted premise that being respected is critical to one's ability to lead—and that we must *earn* respect over time. Personally, I agree with both of these assertions.

But when I ask someone, as I have done many times, what the key to *earning* another's respect is, the pat answer I usually get troubles me. Yet, I've heard it again and again.

"To earn respect from others, you must respect others."

I'm sorry, but I just don't buy it.

Think with me for a moment. If earning the respect of another is dependent on my respecting others completely, then I must respect everyone to be respected by everyone? Well, that's simply impossible. I can't do it. The fact is, I *don't* respect everyone. And neither do you.

Let's face it: Some people we encounter in our work and life have absolutely no desire to earn my or anyone else's respect. Yet my success as a leader hinges on whether those same people respect me in the position I occupy. How can a leader deal with such a precarious situation?

77

A Recipe for Respect

First of all, whether we respect an individual or not, that person still deserves to be *treated respectfully*. Not liking or respecting a person (or the position she represents) does not give us the freedom to treat people rudely, callously, or thoughtlessly. Contrary to what we see and hear on television and talk radio these days, mocking, belittling, demeaning, humiliating, talking over, running down, undercutting, and screaming at are never acceptable leadership behaviors. Such tactics may appear to work well for media personalities, politicians, and antagonists of all stripes bent on building support from one group by alienating another. But such tactics never work for leaders whose goals are to build consensus and grow camaraderie within the various groups they have been tapped to lead.

Second, we shouldn't really view respect as some sort of "I'll scratch your back if you'll scratch mine" reciprocal agreement. Earning leadership respect is not the same thing as "You bought my lunch last time, so I'll pick up the tab this time" or "They sent our Belinda a wedding gift three years ago, so we must reciprocate and send their Robert a gift when he marries later this year." Those are examples of displaying common courtesy. Earning respect, however, is more important than adhering to social conventions—and infinitely more difficult.

The Recipe for Earning Respect

I love biscuits made from scratch. Luckily, I grew up around excellent scratch biscuit makers. As a child, I remember sitting in the kitchen transfixed as I watched either my mother or grandmother working culinary magic. Admittedly, the ingredients they relied on were basic staples found in virtually every kitchen: flour, salt, baking powder, milk, and shortening. However, the artistry resided not in the ingredients, but in the skillful combination of these ingredients.

I've discovered that earning others' respect is a lot like making homemade biscuits. Surprising as it may seem, becoming respected doesn't require a wide range of ingredients. In fact, I believe only three critical elements are required. However, like any premier biscuit baker, knowing when and how to apply the master's touch in combining those basic ingredients ultimately determines the difference between respect earned and opportunity squandered.

Remember, no single one of these ingredients can carry the load alone. You need all three to successfully earn others' respect. Understanding them first, then understanding how to make them work in concert with one another, is where leadership mastery begins and where respect is sure to be earned.

Respect Ingredient #1: Consistency

We all recognize that consistency is important in business. For customers or clients to have confidence in the goods and services we provide, we must offer consistent quality, delivery, responsiveness, follow-up, support, and service. Without confidence in our ability to do this, customers are forced to look elsewhere to have their needs met. This same ground rule holds true for followers in search of a leader.

If a leader develops a reputation for being inconsistent in either words or actions, followers eventually lose confidence in this person's ability to lead effectively. As a result, followers will see no alternative but to search for leadership elsewhere. Remember one of this book's primary assumptions—that followers desire to be led. We all want a leader. In fact, we *need* a leader to help us navigate our way through those perilous areas where we don't know how to help ourselves. But leadership inconsistency can derail all that. Consider the following simple illustration of how fundamental consistency in words and actions can impact our ability to lead more effectively.

Let's assume you know you've made a significant professional mistake that no one, including your leader, has yet discovered. It's not your intention to cover up the mistake or blame someone else for it. You know what you need to do: The first step in resolving the problem is to fess up. You need to come clean with your boss first, then with others your error might affect. And that's exactly what you resolve to do.

You say to yourself, "First thing tomorrow morning, I'm going to step up and do the right thing. I'm going to my boss's office and bring him up to speed on my mistake and all the ramifications associated with it."

You awake with the same resolve the next morning. You anticipate that the conversation with your boss is not going to be a pleasant one. But you're convinced it's the right thing to do, and you're resolved to do it.

You arrive at work, a slight sense of dread washing over you. Nevertheless, you're committed. You head down the hallway. As you approach your boss's office, you notice a colleague exiting. As you pass briefly, you ask a simple, but direct question.

"What kind of mood is he in?"

Your colleague looks up rather dejectedly, points toward his backside, and responds sarcastically, "Well, at least he shouldn't be too hungry when you get in there—he just chewed on this pretty good."

So what do you do now? That's right! If you're like most of us, you will probably do an about-face right there in the hallway, retreating to the perceived security of your office.

There's no reason to bother him right now, you think. *My problem will still be around later today . . . or even tomorrow. I'll just come back when he's in a better mood.*

The first question to consider is who is at fault in this scenario? We certainly can't ignore your burden of responsibility. After all, you made the mistake; therefore, you have an obligation to make your boss and other colleagues aware of it. Remember, as a leader, you must be willing to take action—to do the things that need to be done, even if they're unpleasant or uncomfortable.

But I think there's more fault to go around here. Your boss also bears a measure of responsibility. Because of his inconsistency—in this case, his moodiness—you opt to avoid discussing a problem that you know you should have brought to light earlier. Actions that should have been instituted to deal with correcting the problem—and resolving the issues that it creates—are unnecessarily delayed. Remember, consistency is not a concept; it's a personal discipline.

The Wisest Man in Princeton, Kentucky

It was an exciting time for my wife, Susan, and me. We had advanced to the final trimester in anticipation of our first child's arrival. We experienced all the predictable emotions that soon-to-be-parents feel—excitement, anticipation, and our fair share of predelivery nerves. The fact that we were living in Florida at the time—more than 700 miles from our immediate family in Kentucky—only served to put a fine point to the fact that we were truly on our own.

About that time, I had to make a solo return trip to my hometown of Princeton, Kentucky, a community of about 6,500 residents where almost everyone knows everyone else—and their business.

I was walking down West Main when I heard someone whistle. I looked up to see a familiar face across the street, motioning for me to join him. I crossed the street to be greeted warmly by the local barber. Herb was my father's contemporary and a dear friend to our entire family. I was genuinely glad to see him.

"Boy, it's good to see you," he said affectionately. "How long have you been in town?"

"I just got in," I responded.

"Well, I understand you're gonna be a daddy pretty soon. I know you're excited," he said enthusiastically.

Before I knew what was happening, I heard myself utter two unplanned words in response.

"I was," I said.

"Was?" Herb responded incredulously. Then, without missing a beat, he quickly added, "Boy, don't you want that baby?"

I paused momentarily. Why had I blurted those words out to Herb? Why? I wasn't sure of the reason, but I knew for sure that Herb was standing there, awaiting my response.

"Herb, of course I want the baby. But this is a huge responsibility, and I don't know anything about being a father," I confessed.

Herb straightened up and smiled.

"Son, I'm gonna tell you something right now, and it doesn't matter if you have one child or a dozen children, if you remember and practice this one thing, you'll be a great father."

One thing? I thought. *Surely I can do* one thing!

Herb continued: "You may not always be able to predict what your child will do, or say, or think. But you're the father; your child must always be able to predict with certainty what you will do, or say, or think. That way, he can adapt and adjust his behavior to yours."

Herb spoke those words to me more than a quarter century ago. But they have proven their value again and again over the years, serving me well as I worked to be a better father. They have also served me well as I have worked to be a better leader.

These words were so crucial because they highlight the reason leadership consistency is so critical to the process of earning respect: A leader's consistency provides a *predictive foundation* from which followers can begin to think, decide, and act. If a leader does not establish that foundation, he or she—albeit unintentionally—creates confusion, uncertainty, and potentially chaos in followers' minds.

As strange as this may seem when you first read it, I have suggested before that if you are *occasionally* a thoughtless jerk, it's better to be a thoughtless jerk all the time—consistently! At least that way, followers will always know what to expect and be better able to adapt and adjust their actions and behaviors accordingly.

Respect Ingredient #2: Quality Decision Making

We have hopefully established by this point the importance of consistency for leaders as they intentionally turn their attention to earning respect. But as I mentioned earlier, consistency alone will not win the day. Someone could be consistently wrong, consistently malicious, or even consistently absent. Such consistent behavior might allow us to predict the future and prepare accordingly, but it would not earn respect. And again, to earn others' respect, all three ingredients must work together.

Therefore, the second ingredient in my recipe for respect is the ability to make quality decisions. Please note that I did not say *perfect* decisions; I said *quality* decisions. It's impossible to make a perfect decision without perfect knowledge of the future. And since no one I know is omniscient, we should not expect perfection in our own or in other people's decision making.

But quality decision making is different. You and I can consistently put ourselves in positions to make good quality decisions by establishing some basic standards up front—then following those standards habitually.

"Honey, How Far?"

I had just announced a break during a public seminar I was leading. As most of the program participants were streaming out of the room, I noticed one young woman heading in my direction. She extended her hand and smiled broadly.

"Mr. Van Hooser, I wanted to tell you how much I'm enjoying this training session."

"Well, thank you," I said as we shook hands.

"I've especially enjoyed the stories you've shared to illustrate your points," she continued. "Are you interested in hearing a story that taught me a great deal?"

"I'd love to."

She began her story with great enthusiasm.

"It was the week of my first car date. I must've been about 15 years old. This was the first time a boy had ever called my house and asked me to go out on a real live date. To my utter surprise and amazement, my parents granted their permission. I was overjoyed!

"As the week before my first date unfolded, I could think of little else. I must admit, I tried on every piece of clothing I owned in search of the perfect outfit. And I spent hours thinking about my hair. I wanted it to look just right!

"My parents were very understanding through this entire episode. They didn't tease or lecture me. They seemed intent on letting me fully enjoy the experience.

"Two nights before the date was to take place, my mother and I were clearing away the dinner dishes. As I carried an armload of plates toward the sink, my mother spoke. 'Darling, come in here and sit down at the table. I want to talk to you.'

"Immediately, I knew where this conversation was going. I'd been wondering when I would get the 'sex' talk. But I was ready. As I deposited dishes in the sink and made my way toward the table, I decided to act as if I knew absolutely nothing. I planned to listen to whatever she had to tell me, nod innocently, and get our talk over with as quickly and painlessly

A Recipe for Respect

as possible. I was confident in my ability to handle this situation. I sat down across the table from my mother and our eyes met.

"'Yes, Mother, what would you like to talk about?'

"My mother smiled.

"'You're excited about this weekend, aren't you?'

"'Yes, ma'am, I am.'

"'Well, you ought to be. Play close attention to your thoughts and feelings. Maybe you'll have a daughter one day, and you can share this special experience with her as she prepares for her first big date. But, in any event, I have another question.'

"'What is it, Mother?'

"The smile left my mother's lips. She stared at me intently.

"'Honey, how far are you willing to go with that young man this weekend?'

"The words were simple but difficult to hear. Their impact struck with the power of a lightning bolt. I was shocked. I didn't know what to say. I'd never known my mother to speak so directly, especially on such a delicate subject. I stuttered, desperately trying to gather my thoughts. Finally, out of desperation, I spoke, simply trying to buy more time to think.

"'Mother, I don't know what you mean,' I lied.

"My mother simply repeated the question. She knew that I knew what she meant. Her gaze was unrelenting. Finally, I was forced to admit the obvious.

"'Mom, I don't know,' I said honestly.

"Without even a moment's hesitation, my mother responded. 'Honey, you've got to decide right now. Because if you don't, when you find yourself in that young man's arms this weekend, you'll go further than you intended to go—and you'll have to deal with the guilt and repercussions of your indecision afterwards.'"

The simplicity, truth, and power of the young woman's story immediately struck me. And it wasn't just for its significance as a coming-of-age experience between a mother and her daughter. The story's significance has unmistakable implications for leaders.

If we, as leaders, don't know how far we are (or are not) willing to go when faced with the inevitable professional decisions we must make, we, too, may find ourselves dealing with the frustration, the guilt, and the negative repercussions of decisions we make in the heat of the moment. Successful leadership grows from a well-developed, preestablished personal foundation—a foundation based on quality decisions made.

And these quality decisions require that each of us, as individual leaders, consider where we stand on issues (and what we stand for) before we're forced to make decisions.

Respect Ingredient #3: Interacting with Others

As the 1970s rock musician Meat Loaf reminded us in a memorable line from one of his rock ballads, "Two out of three ain't bad."

Well, 67 percent of the intended goal might not be bad from a rock-and-roller's perspective, but from the perspective of a leader trying to earn the respect of those around us, two out of three just won't get us to where we want and need to be.

Assuming you master the arts of consistency and quality decision making, I'll admit that you'll be well on your way to earning the respect of virtually everyone you encounter. And in all candor, with those two out of three under your belt, you'll already be farther down the road than most people ever get. But this book is dedicated to what *Leaders Ought to Know,* not to what the average person who is interested in being a follower, not a leader, ought to know. Therefore, two out of three is simply not good enough; you're not quite there yet. There's still that issue of interacting with others to contend with, especially others who are different from you in some way.

Here's a thought to kick around for a minute or two: Think about the people you work with. How many of them can simply make you smile when they cross your mind? Chances are, these people are usually positive, upbeat, and willing to lend a helping hand. They're easy to talk to, and they're interested in you and what you have to offer. Simply being in their presence tends to make you happier, encouraged, and more optimistic about the future.

So have you thought of a few folks who fit the bill? If you have, you're lucky. In fact, I believe it's more than luck. If you believe there's a God in heaven—as I do—I suggest you take time regularly to thank God for those very people who make your life better and more pleasant, because those people are nothing short of a blessing to you. Unfortunately, you don't get extra credit as a leader for loving the lovable.

Take another minute to think about the people you work with one more time—and this time, imagine someone that just seems to bring out the worst in you. These are probably the people who are consistently negative, caustic, and argumentative. They're difficult to approach when you need help, and they are far more interested in their own issues than in what others might be dealing with. Even on one of their few good days, if they walked into your office and said, "Good morning," you can imagine finding yourself thinking, *I'd like to slap the taste right out of your mouth!*

Okay, so maybe I went a tad too far there; perhaps you're not the type to fantasize about physical aggression. Even so, I'll bet you understand what I mean. Let me remind you again that you don't get extra credit for loving the lovable. But this time you're in luck. You *do* get double credit in life for loving—and working with and leading—those who are not so lovable.

I'm a collector of quotes. I have collected many that have impacted me in one way or another over the years. If asked for my single favorite quote, though, there would be little hesitation in my response. There is a quote attributed to Abraham Lincoln, the sixteenth president of the United States—and a native Kentuckian, I might add—that I think *Leaders Ought to Know.*

"I don't like that man," Honest Abe admitted, before adding, "I think I need to get to know him better."

That's the type of leader I aspire to be—the type of leader who can be honest about his feelings toward a particular individual and then soldier on anyway, determined to build a better leader-follower relationship.

Of course, the average manager or supervisor is more apt to say, "I don't like that man or woman. I think I will ignore them, separate myself from them, or reassign them." Most would do anything but work to understand this individual and

89

A Recipe for Respect

earn their respect. But remember: This book is not written for the *average* manager or supervisor. This book is for the extraordinary manager or supervisor who is committed to doing everything he or she can to become a better leader. This book is written for *you*.

Wrapping It Up

I'm not going to kid you; there is nothing easy about earning respect. It takes hard work, commitment, selflessness, personal sacrifice, attention to detail, and many other rare human attributes as one strives to be consistent, make quality decisions, and interact with all kinds of people. But I can promise something to those dedicated few who are willing to make such a commitment and then follow through: The long-term benefit of your efforts will be worth it. You will be guaranteed to earn the respect of those around you because you have accomplished what most can't—and what others simply won't.

Chapter 5

Honesty and Other Truths

Ground Rule #5

Leaders don't play loose with the truth;

Leaders lead from a position of unquestioned honesty.

The Truth about Honesty

Not long ago, I was having a conversation with a colleague of mine. We were talking about various people we knew in common when my friend asked pointedly, "Do you know so-and-so?" The person he mentioned was not a friend of mine, but was someone with whom I was vaguely familiar.

"Yeah, I know who you're talking about," I confirmed. "But I can't say that I know him well."

"Well, if you knew him like I know him, you'd know that he tells the truth just often enough to keep everyone confused."

The line was delivered with a dry, matter-of-fact tone that I initially found to be rather humorous. I remember thinking, *what an interesting turn of a phrase—"just often enough to keep everyone confused."*

But then, as the humor passed, I began thinking about the serious impact his words had. Leaders should never be known for *causing* confusion. My friend had felt compelled to provide an unsolicited warning—albeit one housed in a sheath of humor—concerning another person's questionable relationship with the truth (to put it generously). When anyone—but *especially* those of us in leadership positions—somehow earns a reputation for playing loose with the truth, others inevitably will hear about it. As a result, our leadership positions, reputations, and effectiveness are sure to suffer. Believe me. I know.

The Scheduler's Position

I looked up after hearing a knock at my office door and recognized my visitor immediately. Gary and I were coworkers at the same manufacturing plant. He was in inventory control, and I was the employee relations supervisor. Though we were about the same age, both of us in our mid-20s at the time, Gary had been with the company for two or three years longer.

There were two things in particular that stood out about Gary. First, he had this strange habit of treating me with an unusually high level of respect, occasionally bordering on deference. A number of times in conversation he had actually referred to me as "sir"—as in "yes, sir" or "no, sir" in response to some basic question I had asked. That always seemed odd to me. I certainly didn't expect such treatment. I supposed at the time that such behavior was his way of showing his respect for my position.

The second thing about Gary was that he was unfailingly polite. Even standing before me at that moment, his politeness was on display.

"C'mon in and sit down, Gary," I offered.

"No, thanks, I'll only be here a minute. I don't mean to bother you. I know how busy you must be," he said. "I just have a real quick question, if you don't mind."

"Sure, what is it?" I asked.

"Have y'all made a decision on that scheduler's position?"

I knew immediately what he was asking.

It was our company policy to post all job openings. The process was simple: The job, along with a brief description, was posted on the bulletin board in the employee break room. Interested employees signed their names to the job posting form. There were no guarantees that signing the posting would result in a job. The only guarantee was an interview.

Several weeks earlier, I had posted an open job. Gary, as well as several other employees, had signed the job posting form indicating their interest. Subsequently, a group of managers that included me had interviewed each of them. But we hadn't communicated a decision after completing the interviews.

Now, one of the job candidates was standing before me, asking where the process stood. His was a legitimate question: "Have y'all made a decision on that scheduler's position?"

It's crystal clear to me today, 30 years later, what the right thing for me—an aspiring leader—was to do in such a situation. But on that day, in that moment, without prior thought or preparation, the fog of immediacy enveloped me.

I knew the answer to his question. The simple, honest answer was, "Yes, we've made a decision (and it's not going to be you)." That's what I should've said. That's what I wish I would've said. But that's not what I said. Not by a long shot. Instead, I heard myself utter these words: "Umh, well no, we haven't quite made a decision yet."

This is just a little white lie, and a necessary one—right? What else could I say at that moment?

"We expect to make a final decision in the next couple of weeks, though."

This little lie should give me wiggle room to cover that first little lie.

"But as soon as we decide, you can be sure you'll be the first to know."

While I'm at it, why not build some personal rapport? He'll probably forget this little promise anyway.

Have you ever noticed how the second lie is a bit easier to tell than the first one? I didn't wake up that morning thinking to myself, *I wonder how many people I can lie to today.* But because I hadn't awakened with the continuing affirmation, *I will not, under any circumstances, lie to anyone today,* there I was, lying to Gary—in bunches.

Once my trifecta of untruths had been delivered, the ball was in Gary's court. What do you think he did with it? If you think he might have questioned my truthfulness and candor, right then and right there, you would be wrong. I'm sure Gary was not channeling Ernest Hemingway in that moment; nevertheless, a Hemingway quote applied: "The best way to find out if you can trust someone is to trust them." I'd never given Gary prior reason to *not* believe me, so he did.

On the other hand, if you think Gary probably stayed true to his character and acted like the ever-polite gentleman he was, you would be right. Incredibly enough, he *apologized* to me.

"I'm really sorry to have bothered you, Phil. I know you guys are busy, and I'm sure you're doing the best you can. I'm just a little anxious. But I can wait. I appreciate your time," he said. Then he shook my hand and left.

I wish I could say that I was immediately racked with an overpowering sense of guilt and remorse for the lies I'd just told—but to claim that was the case would also be untrue. Instead, as conscienceless and unfeeling as it may sound, I just went about my business, giving the whole matter very little additional thought.

That is, until that afternoon.

Do you believe in coincidence, karma, providence, fate, destiny, comeuppance? Whatever you might call it, I got mine in full measure that afternoon. And I've never forgotten the lesson that came with it.

Four times a year, our employees assembled for a state-of-the-company address that our plant manager led. The address included updates on safety, quality, production, sales, profitability, and the like. It also gave employees an opportunity to ask questions.

I remember exactly where I was standing when the bomb fell. After about 20 minutes of sharing business details, our plant manager opened the floor for questions. A hand shot up on the front row.

"Yeah, any decision yet on that open scheduler's position?" the questioner asked.

No, it wasn't Gary asking the question. There was no need for Gary to ask. He already knew the answer. He'd gotten it

Honesty and Other Truths

earlier in the day from the horse's, um, mouth—right? Therefore, it would've been impolite to ask again. It was one of the other candidates who posed the question to our plant manager. Gary just sat quietly and listened.

Try to imagine the horror and dismay I felt in that moment as I, too, listened to our plant manager. In fact, I could barely believe my ears.

"Yes, we've made that decision," he said. "We actually made it several weeks ago, but we decided not to release the information then. But since we're all here, I see no harm in announcing publicly who our new scheduler is." Then he did so.

At that moment, 399 sets of eyes were securely fixed on the plant manager. One set of eyes—Gary's—found me. And I honestly felt that his eyes could speak to me. They were saying loudly and clearly, *You lied to me, Phil! How could you? You're nothing but a common liar!*

As soon as the meeting ended, I knew what I had to do. I made a beeline straight to Gary. I'd created an unenviable task for myself. I had to try to mend some fences. I had to beg for forgiveness. I had to try to win back Gary's trust and respect.

"Gary, please let me explain," I began. "You caught me at a bad time this morning. . . . I wasn't at liberty to release any information. . . . I didn't want to hurt your feelings. . . . I didn't know what to say to you," and so I rambled on, almost incoherently.

All the while Gary stood stoically, staring at me, saying not a word or showing any emotion. Eventually, I realized I'd begun to repeat myself, so I finished with a final pitifully ineffective plea. "Gary, I hope you can understand the position I was in."

I'd lied to Gary without cause or provocation, and now I was asking Gary—the actual recipient of my lie—to understand my position and forgive me! What gall!

Gary looked at me one last time. He'd heard enough. I don't know what was going through his head. I don't know what he was tempted to say or do. But I remember distinctly what he actually said. As he turned to walk away, he looked over his shoulder at me and, with a dismissive tone, said simply, "Whatever." No shouting, no cursing, no outward display of emotion whatsoever. He was too polite for that. He just walked away, leaving that one word, *whatever,* to ring in my ears.

Leadership Failures

It's no surprise that my relationship with Gary was never the same after that day. The respect he'd shown me and my position previously was gone. I had lost it. I had failed.

I worked at that plant with Gary for another couple of years before my career led me elsewhere.

In the years since, I've lost track of him completely, but I've never forgotten the lesson I learned from that singular encounter. That experience remains with me to this day as one of my most regrettable leadership failures—and one of the best leadership lessons I've ever learned.

I'll remind you that professional failures need not be fatal or final. Our failures can actually serve as lifelong lessons, serving well those we lead, *if* we're willing to learn from them. As that famous American author and humorist Mark Twain once wrote, "Always acknowledge a fault. This will throw those in authority off their guard and give you an opportunity to commit more."

I believe a seedling of truth rests in such humor. As a leader, I've failed more times than I care to recount. And because I'm not yet ready to hang up my leadership spurs, I'm sure more failures await me beyond my current horizon. But over time, I've learned the value of acknowledging my failings and faults to both myself and others, as I try to learn from each one.

I returned to the privacy of my office following that fateful quarterly meeting, crestfallen and intending to lick my wounds, with the possibility of a little personal pity party thrown in for good measure. But then, sitting in the quiet isolation of my office, reality came calling. I realized that the leadership wounds I'd received that day were self-inflicted. No one had made me lie or even suggested that I should. It came too easily for me.

So I decided to make it harder for myself. In my office that afternoon, I made a promise to myself that I've kept until this day and that I intend to keep for the rest of my life. And while it was relatively easy to say, it's proven much harder to keep: I will not lie to my followers.

First of all, I shouldn't be lying because it's wrong. *Leaders Ought to Know* that's reason enough. But second, I—or any other leader—cannot afford the negative repercussions of such a selfish, shortsighted act as personal dishonesty.

So I've committed myself to being honest with my followers. If I'm to fail or suffer professionally, I intend to do so with a clear conscience, not constantly looking over my shoulder and trying to remember what version of the truth I told one person and not the other.

You may be wondering, after 30-plus years, whether it gets any easier to be honest with followers. My personal experience has been that it gets eas*ier* over time, but it never gets easy.

You may also be wondering if being honest, as a leader, means you must tell everyone everything you know or to which you have access. Of course not! The ability to maintain appropriate confidentiality regarding information available to you has been and always will be a critical element of leadership. Leaders of all ranks and ilks regularly possess knowledge of confidential information that they either cannot or should not share with others, for any number of reasons.

And that's when the games begin.

The Honesty Game

For the record, I would do nothing intentionally to diminish the importance of honesty in this serious discussion of what *Leaders Ought to Know*. However, I readily admit my willingness to do almost anything in an effort to emphasize and anchor the importance of honesty in this same discussion of what *Leaders Ought to Know*. So I've devised a game that I call the honesty game.

Game Contestants

The honesty game pits leaders against followers.

1. *Leaders* are defined as those individuals in possession of and charged with managing confidential information on the entire organization's behalf.

2. *Followers* are defined as those individuals wishing to have immediate, unfiltered, and unrestricted access to that confidential information for their own individual, often unstated, purposes.

Objectives of the Game

The honesty game has dual objectives:

1. To build and maintain an ongoing positive, productive, and trusting working relationship between leaders and followers.

2. To manage information flow between leaders and followers employing the most honest, considerate, and efficient methods possible—all the while protecting the confidentiality and integrity of the information to be shared and the individuals it impacts (directly or indirectly).

Rules of the Game

The honesty game has differing rules for the participants:

1. Rules for leaders

    a. Work with followers to accomplish the organization's established objectives.

    b. Consistently share timely and appropriate information with followers in an ongoing effort to help them

Leaders Ought to Know

do their jobs most effectively, while building and maintaining a positive, trusting working relationship with those same followers.

c. Do not, under any circumstances, reveal or share confidential information with followers that could be judged to violate existing laws, rules, regulations, or policies or that in any way could be construed as being:

   i. Illegal

   ii. Immoral

   iii. Unethical

   iv. Highly impractical

2. Rules for followers

   a. None.

   b. In an effort to secure desired confidential information from leaders, it's acceptable and expected that followers will do whatever they deem necessary and appropriate, including but not limited to:

   i. Pressing: "Oh, c'mon, you might as well go ahead and tell me. You know I'm just going to keep asking, day after day, never letting up until you finally give in and tell me what I want to know."

   ii. Begging: "Please tell me what's going on. Just this once and I'll never ask again. You know you can trust me. Whatever you tell me will stay right here. I won't tell a soul, I swear."

Honesty and Other Truths

iii. Slamming or guilting: "How long have we known each other? Fifteen years, that's how long! And now you won't even share a little information with me? Well, I guess I see what this friendship really means to you."

iv. Threatening: "I'll tell you right now—if you won't do me this one little favor and tell me what's going on, well then, don't ever come asking for my help again, because I can promise you, you won't get it. You can bet that I won't forget."

Losing the Game

Followers really can't lose, since they never really expect the leaders to share restricted, confidential information in the first place. If followers' attempts don't succeed, they tend to consider themselves to be no worse off for trying. Leaders, on the other hand, can definitely lose the honesty game—along with their future ability to lead—if they prove themselves unwilling or unable to appropriately manage confidential information entrusted to them.

Winning the Game

Followers will consider themselves winners if they are able to persuade leaders to relinquish any amount of confidential information that they (the followers) didn't have or expect to receive.

Leaders can and will come out on top if they are able to appropriately manage confidential information *and* maintain a positive, professional, and trusting working relationship with followers, throughout and following the honesty game. And bonus points are available if they can do this despite followers' most aggressive attempts. Those bonus points come in the form of heightened respect from these very same followers.

It occurs when the followers come to a point where they consciously think: *My leader wouldn't share inappropriate, confidential information* with *me, despite my continued attempts to persuade him or her otherwise. Therefore, I can now trust that she or he will not share inappropriate, confidential information* about *me—despite others' continued attempts to have him or her do so.*

At such a point as this in the honesty game, appropriate bonus points have been earned and deposited automatically into your leadership account.

Time Frame of the Game

It's continuous; in fact, it's under way right now. Time-outs are not allowed. Get started!

The Zipper Factor

What do you think of my rendition of the honesty game? *Not based in reality,* you think? *There are no real-world applications for the premise of the game,* you imagine? I beg to differ. Real-world, commonsense examples of this premise are all around us and have been for as long as there have been leaders and followers.

I can remember a dinner I had with a labor attorney friend almost 30 years ago. Despite the significant lapse of time between then and now, the conversation remains crystal clear in my mind. Why? Because of the example he shared of how a brilliant leader can (and did) win the trust of his followers by *not* telling them what they desperately wanted to know.

My friend, Richard, worked for a large law firm in Atlanta that provided specialized legal services to companies and organizations facing high-risk labor issues. Richard was especially proficient in leading nonunion organizations through the legal maze that accompanies uninvited unionization attempts in the United States. Over salad, Richard shared a story about an interaction he'd had with a client several years before. I think it perfectly illustrates how a well-intentioned leader can win the honesty game.

An independent, American zipper-manufacturing facility had been purchased by a large Japanese entity. As to be expected, the purchase created a considerable amount of immediate uncertainty within the local workforce. What would happen to the plant and those working there now? Would it be expanded, consolidated, or closed completely? What would happen to the employees if it remained open? Would the new owners honor their jobs and seniority? Would wages and benefits remain the same? Would new management enact new policies and procedures? What future plans did the new owners have for this remote operation?

From the employees' perspective, there were far more questions being asked than answers being offered. Uncertainty gave way to suspicion and dread in countless employees' minds. Some naturally began to fear the worst.

About that time, certain individuals seized the opportunity that this mood of doubt and insecurity created to launch a local union organization drive. Some employees within the company saw future union representation as their sole means of long-term security, while the new owners saw such a move as a blatant sign of distrust and disrespect. Members of the incoming management team felt as if they had not been afforded the opportunity to win the local workforce's trust and respect. Tensions grew as the union drive moved forward.

Eventually, a date for the local union election was set. As that day drew near, those supporting and those opposed to the union worked feverishly to prepare their final presentations and personal remarks for employees in an effort to make their respective cases and influence undecided voters. Emotions were running extremely high.

The Japanese parent company had hired Richard's law firm. Richard, meanwhile, had been personally assigned the task of helping guide the process internally, as well as supporting the general manager in charge. The general manager was native-born Japanese and had been reassigned to this American facility at the time of the acquisition.

"I want tell employees vote no for union. We all family. We take care of them with more raises," said the general manager to Richard in his broken English, during a closed-door strategy session.

"I'm sorry, sir," replied Richard. "You just can't say that here. In America, it's illegal for management to make any economic promises to employees before a union election. Such promises could be seen as an attempt by management to buy votes."

Honesty and Other Truths

"No buy votes," the general manager replied adamantly. "Together build company. We invest in people," he asserted.

"I understand, sir. But as your legal representative, I must advise you not to mention raises during any employee meetings in advance of the union election. It will almost certainly be construed as an attempt to sway the election results. I must tell you, there could be serious repercussions if you do otherwise," Richard warned.

But the gentleman was adamant. Though he recognized his halting English could be a potential detriment to his all-American audience, the general manager was determined to be the face and voice of the parent company. He would stand and share important information—with his own mouth—that the workforce could use to make a better informed decision.

Richard, therefore, worked closely with the general manager to sculpt a scripted, appropriate, and, most important, *legal* presentation to deliver to employees. Nevertheless, Richard could not fully relax. He recognized that it was entirely possible that the general manager would venture off script at some point. Richard admitted to having grave concerns.

It was the day before the scheduled union vote. Plant employees crammed into the meeting venue for the general manager's presentation. At the appropriate time, the GM strode on stage and faced the audience. He proceeded, in a measured, deliberate manner, to deliver his prepared comments. His words echoed his beliefs. He shared that his company had made a significant investment in this facility because they saw great potential. They looked forward to working together to develop that potential, thus realizing significant future success for all team members. The GM finished his remarks by stressing his belief that those successes could be even greater and secured more readily without the involvement of a third party, the union. With his prepared comments delivered, he paused momentarily, and then asked for questions.

"Yeah, I've got a question," said someone in the audience. "We want to know, if we don't vote for the union—will management give us all a raise?"

The inherent danger in the general manager's anticipated response to the question was quite real. Any comments he made about future raises following the election were tantamount to an implied promise—or threat—on the part of company management. Any such response could easily manifest itself in an unfair labor practice charge being filed against the company. The future of the company's relationship with the government and its own employees rested completely in the hands of the general manager.

The GM looked directly at the questioner. Once the question was finished, he paused briefly and surveyed the assembled group. Every eye and ear in the audience was trained on him in anticipation of his response. Eventually, the general manager began his slow, calculated response.

"Information up to here," he said, using a hand gesture positioned just below eye level, before dramatically adding, "but lawyer say zipper here!" He concluded his answer by lowering his hand slightly while making a sweeping motion across his mouth as if to zip his lips.

Brilliant! Absolutely brilliant!

Of course, the audience wanted more information than the general manager ultimately provided. But legally, he gave them all he could. Nevertheless, down deep, I believe the audience understood—and I'm betting at least some of them appreciated his handling of the situation.

Though the story is not a recent one—by Richard's accounting, it's now more than 30 years old—it still packs commonsense educational and instructional value for leaders today. At the very least, it reminds leaders everywhere that it's difficult to say the wrong thing if your lips are zipped.

Brutal Honesty

I must be careful. It would be easy for me to finish this discussion regarding the value of honesty by reiterating that honesty is the most important characteristic of leadership and simply leave it at that. I certainly believe that to be true. If you don't have honesty at the heart of the leader-follower relationship, it's hard to imagine how it could ever flourish. But there is also a warning note that I must sound.

Though clearly important, honesty can also be extremely hurtful if used inappropriately. It can result in lasting, even permanent damage to that same leader-follower relationship. On far too many occasions over the years, I've seen men and women in significant leadership positions opt to use honesty like a chain saw instead of a scalpel. They rightfully (too often, even *proudly*) argue that they were just delivering some sort of unassailable truth—a truth that others appeared unable or unwilling to deliver. In the process, they casually—and perhaps intentionally—ignore the subtleties of appropriate, follower-focused truth telling. The long-term results are often hurt feelings, fractured relationships, and possibly even vindictive responses.

Such undesirable outcomes may begin like this.

A group of managers or supervisors sit around a conference room table discussing some organizational obstacle that must be overcome. Often that obstacle involves some sort of human element. As the conversation builds and continues and the managers discuss how best to deal with this particular individual, one in the group gets his belly full of the whole affair.

"I don't understand why we're wasting all this time!" he exclaims. "We all know that Bonnie's the problem. But apparently, you're afraid to tell her the truth. Well, someone needs to tell her and I'm not afraid! I'll go tell her right now."

With that, the individual rises to leave. Unfortunately, no one raises a hand to stop him. We let the person go on a fool's journey without a word of direction or caution.

A few minutes later, the same individual reappears in the doorway. Obviously proud of himself, he puffs out his chest, hikes up his pants, and announces defiantly, "That message has been delivered. That problem has been fixed. Now let's move on to more important issues, like managing this business!"

Well, the message may have been delivered, but are we absolutely sure the problem has been fixed? Or is it possible— actually, more realistic—that even more problems have been created?

A manager or supervisor who manages things—physical, financial, or technical resources—might be able to make the bull-in-the-china-shop approach work. But when leading people, discretion is the better part of valor.

Please understand that I'm not suggesting, not even for one moment, that leaders should avoid difficult conversations when necessary. We must communicate the truth, even during difficult circumstances. But *how* we communicate difficult truths can make the long-term difference between a positive, trusting leader-follower relationship and a continuing struggle with follower interaction, engagement, and motivation. And follower motivation is a worthy goal.

Leaders Ought to Know

Chapter 6

Two Motivational Truths

Ground Rule #6

Leaders don't motivate followers;

Leaders search for the wants and needs that motivate followers.

What Supervisors and Managers Want to Know

When I'm working with supervisors and managers directly, I frequently start the interaction with a simple question: "If you could gain one thing in particular from our time together, what would it be?"

My question's intent should be obvious. When I know up front what my audience (my followers) want or need, I can focus on shaping our interaction to specifically address those individual needs. Once I've successfully helped satisfy their needs, they're almost always more positive, receptive, engaged—motivated as a result.

Please read the previous two paragraphs one more time. In reality, they're not about how I approach my job—they're about how you should approach yours. Within those two paragraphs rests a significant truth about human motivation.

Let me reposition the statements ever so slightly, and maybe that significant truth will make more sense to you:

If *you* know up front what *your* followers want or need, *your* focus should be on shaping *your* interaction with them to specifically address those individual needs. Once *you've* successfully helped them satisfy *their* needs, you can expect *your* followers to be more positive, receptive, engaged—motivated.

Doesn't that sound like the essence of a motivated workforce to you?

Help Me Motivate My People

Having posed that opening question to a great many supervisors and managers over the years, the variety of responses I've received can be dizzying. Responses like:

- "I really need someone to help me verbalize the vision I have for my group."

- "Could you show me how to make more decisive and assertive decisions?"

- "I'd love to know any tricks or techniques that would help me become a better listener."

- "Can you help me overcome my fear of confrontation?"

These actual responses (along with a long list of others not included here) highlight some legitimate leadership issues that deserve attention and instruction. However, I've discovered that for every "better listener" or "more decisive" request, there will eventually be 3, 5, even 10 times that number of requests begging for help in another specific area: "Phil, will you please tell me how to motivate my employees?"

I've heard that singular plea more times than I can count. Motivating their followers is a leadership challenge that's baffled and perplexed dedicated supervisors and managers for generations. Conscientious leaders lay awake at night wondering what they can do to or for their employees to compel those employees to exert more effort and produce better results.

Desperate as many may be for a definitive answer to a personal motivational dilemma, honesty dictates that I tell you now what I've had to tell them for years. "Unfortunately, I can't tell you how to motivate your employees or followers. I wish I could, but I can't. It's not within my power, or anyone else's, to do so."

I've watched anxious listeners process my words and seen disappointment register on their faces as a result. Coming to the realization that we have little or no direct control over the motivation of another can be very discouraging, even for the most dedicated leader. The thought of being unable to encourage someone to do what we want or need him to do can create a sort of black hole in our leadership psyche.

We start to worry. *How will I ever get my job done with unmotivated employees? I've always heard that people can be motivated. So why can't I be the one who motivates them?*

Two Motivational Truths

Motivational Theories Abound

While I was an undergraduate business student in the mid-1970s, one of my professors wheeled a cart holding a dual-reel, 16mm film projector into class one day. If you're under the age of 30, I suggest you cease reading temporarily and Google "antique film projectors" to get a visual image of the contraption I'm referencing. It may take some obscure YouTube posting for you to really appreciate the incessant operational hum of that particular machine. I'm confident that relentless mechanical purr was the root cause for tens of thousands of in-class student naps—and I'm betting at least a half-point drop in student grade point averages around the world.

But on this particular day, the film's subject matter kept me wide awake. During a 45-minute film presentation, I was introduced to the behavioral and motivational theories of one Morris Massey, a sociologist and college professor. In a very entertaining film titled *What You Are Is Where You Were When,* Massey outlined his personal theories regarding the effect values, generational differences, and significant emotional events (SEE) have on human behavior.

I was immediately intrigued. Before that day, I'd spent very little (if any) substantive time thinking about the possibility of cause-effect relationships on human behavior. But in the decades since, I've thought about little else. I've discovered that understanding *why* people do what they do (or don't do what we thought they would or should) is the bedrock foundation on which effective leadership is built.

In Chapter 1, I mentioned "When the student is ready, the teacher appears" and suggested that W. Edwards Deming's work helped lead me to make the single most important professional decision of my life and career. My initial introduction to Massey and his work had a similar effect. Though I couldn't have verbalized that fact at the time, Massey's work served to ready me intellectually and observationally, while creating within me an insatiable curiosity to learn and understand more about what motivates people. As a result, teachers (and various learning opportunities) began to appear in mass—and have continued to reveal themselves to me to this very day.

Sociologists, psychologists, and human behavioral experts of all sorts—bearing such famous names as Abraham Maslow, Frederick Herzberg, Victor Vroom, and, of course, B. F. Skinner—all became familiar to me. Over time, I was introduced to the works of speakers, authors, and thought leaders such as Zig Ziglar, Earl Nightingale, Tom Peters, and Peter Drucker, whose concepts proved to be equally influential. Finally, I've known personal business clients and met entrepreneurs and in-the-trenches leadership practitioners who have influenced my thinking. Individuals bearing names most likely unfamiliar to you—Joe Scarlett, Howard Putnam, Francis Bologna, John Paling, and Jerry Brenda—continue to add a practical, commonsense element to my thinking and leadership approach.

To one degree or another, these individuals' theories, processes, and personal examples—along with hundreds of unnamed and, unfortunately, unaccredited others—have shaped my thinking, work, and the leadership perspectives contained in these pages.

That's not to say that I've *agreed* with everything that each has written or espoused—and neither should you. In fact, on various occasions, I found the opposite to be true. Many of my personal philosophies on leadership, motivation, and human behavior today were shaped—then reshaped—as a result of something I witnessed in real life. And a great deal of these experiences actually ran counter to what the vaunted thinkers of our age had observed in some sterile laboratory, isolated study, or best-selling tome. I have found that observing how behavioral theory meshes with commonsense applications provides a wealth of practical instructional value—where you and I live and work in the real world.

Motivational Truth #1

Considering what I've read, heard, studied, witnessed, and practiced in my first half century of life and work, I'm prepared to make a rather bold statement: that only two motivational truths actually exist. These truths are universal, foundational, and observable wherever you might interact with people—at work, at home, at school, at church—*anywhere.* They were true yesterday, they're true today—and I trust they'll be true tomorrow and forever.

Their implications and importance cannot be overstated, nor should their power be underestimated. Appropriately understanding the premise associated with each can ultimately spell the difference between long-term success and frustrating insignificance in our future leadership undertakings.

But I must warn you, the first motivational truth I'll share flies in the face of conventional wisdom. Countless overzealous motivational speakers—and far too many woefully underprepared bosses—have taught or believed differently than I. They have chosen to believe in some sort of quick, manufactured motivational fix. I simply can't. I can't because I understand the first motivational truth.

That first truth is this: *You can't, I can't, no one can motivate someone to do something they don't want to do!*

During the past 25 years of building my business as a leadership speaker, trainer, and author, not once have I ever promoted myself as being a motivational speaker. Frankly, I would've been terrified to do so. Think about it: What would be expected of me if and when a client hired me as a motivational speaker? To be successful and do the job I was hired to do, every audience member should leave my session personally motivated. It's simply not going to happen. I don't have that kind of mind control over anyone, and neither do you.

However, it is possible to segregate my audience members—and probably your employees as well—into three rather broad categories. Those categories represent the *expectant,* the *curious,* and the *resistant.*

The *expectant* individual is excited by the opportunities made available to her to learn and grow. She appreciates the chance to participate and will do so willingly and actively. She arrives with a positive attitude and an open mind and is ready to get to work. She fully expects to walk away with information, ideas, and techniques that will be of future benefit in her life and work. She gladly engages and involves herself with others. And guess what? Her personal expectations are met—even exceeded—99 percent of the time because she is committed to making it so.

The *curious* participant or employee embraces a different mind-set than the expectant one. He is curious, perhaps a little

Two Motivational Truths

suspicious, about why he's been chosen to participate or assigned a particular job. He wants to know who's in charge or leading the session and what qualifies this person to do so. He's on the hunt to find out the real (in his mind—unspoken or hidden) reason behind the activity. He also wants to know exactly what personal commitments or changes he's expected to make as a result of his participation. He's not a bad person; he's just apt to embrace a wait-and-see attitude until someone can answer all his key questions and until he's convinced that he won't be harmed by his participation. He can and probably will come around, but you can't anticipate that he'll buy in as quickly or as enthusiastically as the expectant-types do.

Finally, we have the *resistant* participant or employee. She arrives at the activity with her mind already made up as to whether she will enjoy or benefit from it (she will not) and whether it's even deserving of her time (it is not). Despite valiant efforts, her session leader or boss can do very little to change her mind. She simply won't allow anyone to alter her mind-set or perspective. Her level of group participation runs the gamut from emotionally distant to outwardly thorny. She can be difficult to work or interact with, and her attitude can (and usually does) negatively impact others—regardless of whether they are expectant, curious, or even resistant like her.

So here's the question of the hour. How would you go about motivating each of these very different personality types? The first group, the expectant folks, shouldn't be hard, since they're pretty much motivated already. You can expect the curious to get where they need to be but in a more cautious way. They don't like to be pushed. Those in the resistant category are simply tough nuts to crack. The truth is that you will never change them. If they change, it will be of their own making—not because you or anyone else forced change on them.

Of course, just because I believe that you can't motivate anyone to do anything they don't want to do doesn't mean that every supervisor and manager I've met shares this belief. Some ignore the fact and push ahead in an effort to satisfy their own agendas. I know—because I've met them.

Motivation versus Manipulation

There I stood, halfway through a three-hour workshop for 35 *Fortune 500* corporate managers. The training room had tables configured in a deep U-shape, with participants sitting on the outside perimeter, each with a clear view of one another. Throughout the session, I'd wandered into, out of, and around the U, sharing my perspectives up close and personal with the participants. It was from inside the U that I shared that first motivational truth with this assembled group.

"The first unassailable truth of motivation is this," I declared authoritatively. "You can't, I can't, no one can motivate someone to do something they don't want to do."

As I confidently made my pronouncement, I was standing inside the U, facing the left side of the room. As I spoke, I noticed participants jotting notes and nodding in casual agreement. Everything seemed to be in order when I noticed a bit of movement out of the corner of my right eye. Instinctively, I turned my body about 45 degrees to the right and looked directly into the face of one of the participants. Unlike his counterparts, he was neither taking notes nor nodding in agreement. This gentleman was leaning back in his seat, arms crossed

119

Two Motivational Truths

over his chest, with a toothy, sarcastic-looking grin fixed across his face. As he smiled, his head shook vigorously, back and forth, in a manner indicating anything but personal agreement.

I immediately realized my precarious position. Had I not turned and faced the man, I might never have known that he'd taken exception to my comment. But the moment I voluntarily faced my newly recognized antagonist, he, I, and everyone in the room knew that a public challenge was inevitable. There was no practical way to avoid it. I couldn't ignore him; his observable level of disagreement demanded my attention.

But how should I handle it? I honestly didn't know what to do or say, much less what to expect from him. I had no fall-back plan, and the clock was ticking. Whether I wanted to or not, I had to respond to him and do it now. I waded in. "Sir, it's possible that I'm wrong, but your body language strongly indicates that you've taken exception with something I've said. Unfortunately, I don't know what it might be. Would you be willing to share your concern with all of us?"

Any first-year law student would've immediately recognized my foolish mistake. *Never* ask a question for which you don't already know the answer! Too late—that card had now been played. I steeled myself for his response.

"Yeah, sure, I'll be happy to share with you," he said confidently, as the entire room watched and listened. "If I'm not mistaken, you just said that you can't, I can't, no one can motivate someone to do something they don't want to do. Did I hear you right?"

He knew he had. He'd repeated my earlier statement verbatim. He was setting the hook. There was no turning back now.

"Yes, that's what I said," I offered hesitantly, not knowing what to expect next.

The manager leaned forward with his forearms on the table and fixed his gaze securely on me. "Well, I'll have you know just two days ago, I gave an employee an assignment that I knew he didn't want to do," said the manager bluntly. He then paused briefly, I believe for effect, before leaning back in his seat, recrossing his arms and delivering his final line: "But you can be sure that I *motivated* him to do it!"

He delivered his last line with a sly smile and just enough haughtiness to create a discernible air of power and personal authority. His attitude and composure let everyone present know that he was in charge—without actually having to say so directly.

With the statement delivered, an uncomfortable silence washed over the room. No one spoke another word. But every eye in the room, which mere seconds before was fixed on the manager in question, was now turned on me in anticipation of my response—possibly, an emotional rebuttal.

As they looked on, I stood still, trying desperately to project an external air of confidence and control. All the while, internally I was searching desperately for the appropriate thing to say or do next—without much success. If you've never had such an experience, then believe me, the front of a crowded room can be a very lonely place when people are awaiting your response, especially if you have no clue as to what that response might be and how others might receive it. And I truly didn't.

To be clear: This manager had not caused me to question the value or veracity of my own belief. I still believed solidly in that first motivational truth. However, I needed to figure out

Two Motivational Truths

how to respond to this detractor in a professional manner without sounding defensive or dismissive of his opinion. I wasn't fooling myself into thinking I could change his mind. Remember: I firmly believe that none of us can motivate any one of the rest of us to do anything we don't want to do. And this man certainly did not want to embrace my viewpoint.

Nevertheless, I was acutely aware of the 34 other souls in that room who might still be making up their minds regarding this motivational truth and its appropriateness.

I was still mentally sorting out how to respond when the alarm on my internal clock sounded: *Time's up! You've got to say something! You can't wait any longer! The silence has become awkward! Speak up! Do it now!*

I admit here and now that when I opened my mouth I had no idea what would come forth. I really didn't know. So I was as surprised as anyone else when I heard what exited through my mouth. "Sir, thank you. I appreciate your candor. But I have one more question, if you don't mind?"

"Sure, ask away," he stated, his confidence on display.

"If you will, please define two words for the group. First, define *motivation,* but while you're at it, go ahead and define *manipulation* as well."

Manipulation Doesn't Pay—It Costs

Unfortunately, I've met and known far too many bosses who've made the same mistake as the manager I've just described. Somehow they fool themselves into believing that if they get an individual to complete a specific task—especially one the person wouldn't have otherwise voluntarily chosen to do—then they (the manager or supervisor) therefore possess some sort of magical, mystical, motivational powers. But it's just not so. And to be oblivious to that fact potentially sets the stage for lasting harm to themselves, their followers, and the organizations they represent.

Never forget that every employee knows where the power rests in their organization; it's not a deep, dark secret. Those who are chosen as supervisors and managers possess the power that comes with the positions they occupy. They may have the organizational power to hire or fire, spend or save, build up or tear down. And employees understand that if their boss tells them to do something, they must do it—or face the predictable consequences that accompany their failure to perform or conform.

But *doing what we're told* doesn't constitute motivation. It's simply observable adherence to authority. But on those occasions when a manager or supervisor—or anyone in a position of power—chooses to wield their organizational power inappropriately, there will most assuredly be predictable consequences to those choices and actions.

So be alert. If you're ever guilty of manipulating (aka unduly influencing, pressuring, coercing, bullying, or intimidating) an individual or group, there is one outcome you can absolutely expect. Once people realize they've been manipulated, they *will*—not might, could, or should—begin figuring out how to get even with the one responsible for the manipulation. And I remind you that *even*, from a manipulated individual's perspective, means "getting even," plus imposing punitive damages! They'll do everything in their power to make you hurt, suffer, and otherwise regret treating them in such a thoughtless, callous, self-serving manner.

123

Two Motivational Truths

So we know that we can't get employees to do what they don't want to do by using some sort of force or coercion. Does that mean that professional motivation is actually some mythical vapor often wished for but never grasped?

No. Motivation is *real* and available to all of us. And the best leaders are the ones who have learned and apply the reality of motivation—as spelled out in the second motivational truth.

Motivational Truth #2

Before I reveal it, however, I want you to think of the most motivated persons you know. They may work for or with you. They may be your children or your spouse. They may be friends or neighbors.

Clearly, I'm suggesting that motivated people are all around us, populating every aspect of our lives. They can be motivated by any number of things—work, school, adventure, hobbies, projects, whatever. The trick for each of us is to identify who they are. Once we do so, then—and only then— are we best positioned to embrace the full reality of the second motivational truth.

The second motivational truth is this: *We are not motivated by what we have; we are motivated by what we don't have but have determined that we want or need.*

Remember—we're thankful for what we have, and we intend to enjoy it. What we have, we're unwilling to give up. But if we already have it, it's no longer a motivational stimulus for us.

Motivation enters the picture once we've set our sights on something we *don't have*—either at all or not enough of—that we *want or need*. Such wants or needs could be physical—a car, a vacation, a promotion—or emotional—power, accomplishment, recognition. The issue really isn't what the thing is. The critical part for leaders to understand is that once we (or our followers) have consciously determined that we want or need something specific, that personal determination serves as the source from which our motivation longing emerges, grows, and expands.

Can We Have a Pool Table?

When I was about seven years old, our family traveled from our home in rural western Kentucky to visit distant relatives living in southern Colorado. What an adventure for a small-town boy from a lower-middle-income family! It was the first time I'd ever traveled to the wild, wild West—and my young imagination was on high alert. We drove almost 3,000 miles round trip. We crossed the granddaddy of all rivers—twice. We sliced our way through America's breadbasket. And we ended up in the shadow of the majestic Rocky Mountains. For me, it was the trip of a lifetime.

But what do I remember most about that trip? A pool table!

We eventually arrived at the country home of my father's well-to-do Colorado cousin. An entire group of unknown relatives were assembled on the porch to greet us. After hugs and handshakes, Dad's cousin turned to his young son (a boy roughly the same age as me) with these simple directions. "Greg, why don't you take Phil up to the rec room?"

Of course, I now realize by *rec room* he was referring to the family's recreation room. However, that's not what I heard

Two Motivational Truths

that day. Not by a long shot. Having never heard the term before and having no knowledge that such a thing actually existed, especially in a private residence, the concept of a private recreation room was completely foreign to me.

What I *thought* I heard him say was, "Greg, why don't you take Phil up to the *wrecked* room?" Now, *that* I understood. How many times in my young life had I already heard my mother declare, "Phil, your room is a wreck"? So I dutifully followed my cousin into the house and up the stairs. I had no expectation other than to see another little boy's room in desperate need of a good cleaning.

Even today, almost five decades later, it's virtually impossible for me to convey the level of shock and amazement I experienced when Greg threw open the door to that room. There before me were two totally unexpected and unforgettable items.

The first was lying on the floor, staring straight up at me. It was a real live (or at least it once had been) bearskin rug. The fur was black and luxurious. The claws were long and ominous. And that head! That magnificent head, with mouth open wide, teeth bared menacingly, seemed to silently communicate the untamed nature of my western surroundings. It was almost more than I could comprehend.

But there was more: Just beyond the bearskin rug stood a full-size *pool table*. At that point, I wasn't sure it was legal to have a pool table in a home. The only ones I'd ever seen came via quick, stolen glances as my mother hustled me past the front door of Papa Bill's Pool Hall on East Court Square in my little hometown, all the while warning me to steer clear of places like that if I knew what was good for me. Now here was my newfound favorite cousin, escorting me into his own personal playroom stocked with forbidden fruit—aka a pool table.

My initial amazement soon gave way to unbridled exuberance. I ignored the untold adventures that lay waiting in the mountains and meadows, on the trails and lakes, with the horses and wildlife just outside the walls of that house. I was transfixed by what awaited me in that one room. For the next several days, all I wanted to do was shoot pool. Game after game, alone or in competition, I played on.

Of course, all good things must come to an end, and so did our visit. Eventually, we headed east once more on that long drive back to Kentucky. My first several hours of the return trip were spent in the backseat of our family station wagon, mentally reliving the events of the previous days. Of all the new experiences I had enjoyed, I reveled most in the joy of being able to play pool virtually nonstop. *Why did it have to stop?* I wondered.

Hmm. Maybe it didn't.

Finally, I summoned the courage to ask the question that had burdened me since shortly after arriving in Colorado. I stood up and leaned forward over the back of the car's front seat (long before the days of mandatory seat belts and child restraint laws). "Daddy, can we get a pool table?" I asked sincerely.

The request was simple and direct. My father's reply was equally direct and definitive. "What? No! Absolutely not! There are a lot of things I can think of that we need a whole lot more than a pool table. Besides, we don't have a room in our whole house big enough for a pool table. Now, I don't want to hear any more about such foolishness."

127

Two Motivational Truths

Matter closed—or so my father must have thought. I didn't discuss it anymore. I just sat back in the seat and fell silent. Some might have wrongly concluded that I was pouting, but I wasn't pouting. I was plotting—and becoming ever more motivated.

I will have a pool table! I don't know when. He may not get me one, but one day I'll have my very own pool table in my house! I promised myself that day.

That thought never left me. Time and again over the years, I revisited the idea of a pool table and when might be the best time to keep that childhood promise to myself.

Almost 30 years elapsed. I was a married father of two when my wife and I determined the time had finally come for us to look for our first house to buy. It was exciting. Susan had her wish list—a particular floor plan, with a certain cabinet configuration, bathrooms, storage, and the like. I, on the other hand, was on the lookout for just one particular feature: a big empty room.

We found the house that suited our needs and wants. We bought it, settled in, and started transforming that house into our home. One of the most exciting days of my life was when my very own brand-new, custom-built pool table arrived and was assembled right before my eyes—in the middle of our living room.

Beginning that day, I shot pool day and night. I hosted pool parties and tournaments for friends and neighbors. Sometimes I just stood and looked at it, caressing the soft felt covering the slate underneath. My enthusiasm continued unabated for several months.

Then one day, without notice, I walked into the room where my pool table stood and took a long look at it.

I distinctly remember a random thought entering my consciousness: *What's so special about that pool table again?* Suddenly, I realized the motivational zest and zeal that had driven me for years to secure a pool table had left me. Was it that I suddenly didn't like playing pool any longer? No, I still enjoyed the game, and I was pleased to have a table readily available. But that driving motivation was gone because I had attained what I had wanted. The reality of the second motivational truth was on full display.

How Can They Sit There and Lie to Me Like That?

Because I had sincerely wanted my own pool table for 30-plus years, I remained motivated to get one. But once I actually had what I'd so desperately wanted and had been driven to secure, the motivational impetus soon diminished. I learned practically firsthand that *we're not motivated by what we have; we're motivated by what we* don't *have but have determined we want or need.*

You shouldn't be surprised when the same sort of thing happens in the workplace. For example, I've heard supervisors and managers complain dozens of times that job candidates had lied to them during job interviews. I've asked them to explain.

"Well, I always ask candidates during interviews what kind of job they're looking for. They tell me they'll do anything. I ask them if they have a particular location or shift preference. They tell me they'll work anywhere and during any shift. I ask them if they'd have any problem with overtime, weekend work, or overnight business travel. They always tell me they'll work all the overtime they can get and they'll gladly travel when asked. And foolish me—I believe them.

"Then, once I hire them and they've worked at their job for a little while, here they come parading into my office complaining about their job, their shift, the overtime, the weekend work, the travel—the whole works. Phil, I'm telling you it won't be but a few months—sometimes just a few weeks— after they're hired that the complaints begin. How can they sit there in the interview and lie to me like that? And for that matter, how can I be so gullible that I can't tell when they're lying to my face?"

I've had to explain to very frustrated bosses many times over the years that the employees they were describing weren't liars. At the time of the interview, they gave completely honest answers to the questions asked. But remember the second motivational truth—*we are not motivated by what we have, we are motivated by what we don't have but have decided we want or need.*

Think with me for a minute. What did these interviewees *not have* at the time of the interview? A job, right?

So they were motivated to get something they *did not have but had decided they wanted or needed.* A job—something that employer had available. In their minds, these interviewees believed what they were saying. They were willing to do anything and work any type of shift to get a foot in the door.

Once they'd secured the job and felt somewhat settled in, the job itself predictably began to lose some of its initial luster. Their current job is no longer motivational to them because they have it. Therefore, their motivation changes, and these relatively new employees start looking around for other jobs (or variations of the one they have) that might be available and that they decide they might want or need more than their current one. You can call that ambition, aspiration, determination, drive, or personal motivation. Most of us would agree that we wish our followers had more of these qualities, not less.

However, harried, overworked bosses have been known to overreact to these normal, even predictable behaviors from their employees. When the employee (new or senior) stops the boss to inquire, complain, or request, the boss—in a moment of frustration—whips out a personal, albeit ineffective motivational comeback.

Looking straight at the employee, the boss shoots back, "You ought to be happy you've got a job!"

The employee is slightly bewildered. *Of course, I'm happy I've got a job*, she thinks. *I'm not talking about what I have; I'm talking about what I don't have but I would like to have.*

And truth be known—these two motivational certainties occupy more of our time and thinking than we may admit.

Remember, you can't motivate me unless I want to be motivated—and I can't motivate you. And I'm motivated as long as I'm working to get something I don't have, that I want, that's important to me—and so are you.

Is That All?

We've now considered the two motivational truths. At this point, I hope you're thinking:

Well, I can't argue with the fact that trying to motivate someone to do something that he or she doesn't want to do is next to impossible.

And I've got to admit, he's right about the other truth, too. There are certainly things I can think of that I've wanted or needed for a long time that have kept me motivated as I've continued to work to get them. On the other hand, I can also think of a number of things that I used to want desperately, that I now have, that I must admit I tend to take for granted. I'm certainly not motivated by them in the same way as I used to be.

But is that all there is to know about motivation and leadership?

No! Now that you've gotten a better handle on the two truths associated with motivation, the time has come to focus on the motivational intricacies that drive people to actually do what they do daily.

Chapter 7

Why People Do What They Do

Ground Rule #7

Leaders can't predict followers' behavior;

Leaders need to know why people do what they do.

The Worst Motivational Speech

"Hey, I need a favor, Phil," my coworker Carl said casually as he slid into a chair in my office.

His words caused me to stop what I was doing and pay close attention.

"What's up?" I asked, with more than a little apprehension.

I didn't normally start conversations with such suspicion. However, I knew Carl. Carl was one of our frontline production supervisors and, frankly, not a very good one. He was likable enough. But as a supervisor, he was terribly hard-headed. He'd been elevated to supervisory status years before—a promotion based more on his production knowledge and seniority than on any kind of ongoing commitment to professional development and leadership competency.

Try as one might to help Carl, it was nearly impossible to get him to listen to any sort of reason or alternative leadership approach—especially if and when it ran counter to his own initial ideas and intentions. Simply put, he wasn't very coachable. Somewhere along the line, Carl had convinced himself that his ideas were always the best ones and that he could get his employees to do anything he asked of them whenever and however he wanted. But I knew better.

As the human resources manager, I'd spent far too many hours in one-on-one conversations with Carl's direct reports. I'd listened again and again as they vented their frustrations about Carl's self-serving, overbearing management style. It was this knowledge that put my suspicions on high alert as he sat in front of me seeking a favor.

Carl apparently sensed my hesitation.

"Oh, don't worry, Phil," Carl offered confidently. "This is easy stuff. This afternoon, just before the end of the shift, I'm gonna have a department meeting," he said, before adding, "I think it's time I give my people a little motivational speech."

I cringed involuntarily. I shifted in my seat, suddenly uncomfortable.

You've gotta be kidding! A motivational speech from you? I thought. *That's just asking for trouble.*

Carl was the last person I would've ever chosen to deliver a motivational speech to his own employees, or anyone else's. And he apparently wanted me to be a willing accomplice. I was unsure of what he had in mind, but I had no intention of participating in it.

"I don't know, Carl," I began. "I can't see how I could be much help to you with that."

"Phil, there's really nothing for you to do," he countered. "I just need you to stand in the back of the room and observe, and then give me some feedback after it's all over. Just let me know how you think it went."

My hesitancy remained. However, I was the HR manager. It was my job to help and support all of the supervisors in any way I could—even Carl. It would've been inappropriate for me to tell Carl, or anyone else, that I was unwilling to observe him doing his job, especially after he'd invited me to do so. So I agreed to participate—but only after securing reassurance that my role in the meeting would just be that of official observer.

That afternoon, I and about 20 or so of Carl's direct reports assembled in the break room. Experienced laborers milled about, each with a keen sense that this 15-minute meeting was all that stood between them and the end of their shift. They were anxious to be on their way but also curious as to what this was all about. They stood or sat stone-faced, scattered about the room, arms crossed, seemingly prepared for whatever was to take place.

Carl began his prepared remarks by reiterating the importance of teamwork and how critical it was for each department member to support one another and, of course, their supervisor—him. He quickly recounted the safety, production, and quality challenges the department had recently experienced, along with a brief reminder of why it was so important to correct these issues.

Carl didn't really share anything new or earth-shattering. Certainly, nothing he'd said so far could be mistaken for a motivational speech. From the perspective of Carl's employees, his presentation was rather formulaic—pretty much what

Why People Do What They Do

they might've expected. After all, they'd seen and heard it all before. No big surprises here.

However, even the most experienced of the group couldn't have predicted what Carl would do next. It all happened so quickly. With no prior warning, Carl stepped out of his predictable formula and into motivational mode.

Grabbing a chair from one of the break room tables, Carl slid it across the tile floor, into the midst of the employees. Following its path closely behind, he leaped up on it as it slowed to a stop. Once standing on the chair, towering above his audience, Carl's melodramatics reached their crescendo.

The scene was truly surreal. It was like watching a car wreck in progress—I didn't really want to watch but couldn't bring myself to look away.

With animated gestures and his high-pitched voice at maximum volume, Carl had every eye, including mine, fixed on him. This was extraordinary by any standard. If his performance had been measured solely on its ability to captivate his audience, he would've received an Oscar.

"Looky here," he squealed, after having listed a number of production goals that had gone unmet in recent days. "The fact is this. Y'all have got to work harder. Because if you don't— they're gonna run me off!"

For a split second, time seemed to freeze as Carl's final words hung in the air. It was as if everyone in the room had hit a mental rewind button and was listening a second time to Carl's impassioned plea, just to be sure they'd actually heard what they thought they'd heard. Once convinced, they started stealing glances at each other one by one—some snickering openly, others whispering.

"Is that really all it takes?" one asked another. "Why has he waited this long to tell us? If we'd known this before, we could've slowed down and done less a long time ago. Then maybe we would've gotten a better leader by now!"

Giving before Getting

Carl's mistake was definitely unforgettable; unfortunately, it's also not terribly unusual. I've seen the same general mistake repeated time and again, though rarely with the theatrics Carl employed.

So what was the fundamental mistake Carl and others too often make? Carl elevated his own personal needs above those of leadership's essential element—his followers. When followers realize their leader is focused on what he can personally garner from the relationship, rather than on what he can do to offer service and take action on behalf of his followers, a very predictable outcome results: Simply put, that leader no longer has followers. At best, he has employees—and not highly motivated ones at that—who, by virtue of the organization's hierarchy, must report to this selfish supervisor, despite their reluctance.

One of my first introductions to the power of motivation occurred while reading Zig Ziglar's seminal book, *See You at the Top*. In it, Ziglar proclaimed, "Anyone can get anything in life they want, if first they are willing to help others get what they want or need."

That statement's truth and commonsense value resonated with me from the moment I read it. Today, more than ever, I believe Ziglar's statement is foundational to what *Leaders*

Why People Do What They Do

Ought to Know about ambition, priorities, motivation, performance, and leadership support.

It's More than Gratitude

You enter a restaurant and happen to see a casual friend or business acquaintance dining alone. She invites you to join her for lunch. You accept the spontaneous invitation. At the end of the lunch, your dining partner unexpectedly picks up the check for both meals. You sincerely resist. There's no reason for her to do that. It's certainly not what you intended. But she insists on paying, stating what a pleasure it was to have had the opportunity to enjoy such good company and conversation.

You leave the restaurant with a full stomach and bolstered self-esteem. Almost immediately, you begin trying to decide how best to return the favor. You make such plans not because you have to or because it's part of some unspoken agreement between you two—but rather because you truly want to give in return for what you received.

Maybe this example is too simplistic for your tastes. Maybe you're thinking, *C'mon Phil, face it, sometimes we all get lucky. I'll just grab my free lunch and move on without wasting too much valuable time thinking about it.* Maybe you think that, but most leaders don't.

Call it a gratitude, karma, reciprocity, lagniappe, or whatever other term works for you, but when someone does something extra or special for us without obvious consideration for themselves, we normally find ourselves wanting to do things to help and support them in return. It's fair to assume that if your employees have total confidence that you, their leader, are working for their best interests every day and in every way, then they, in turn, will be committed to doing their best to support you and your efforts. Not because they *have to,* but because they *want to.*

The Cornerstone Concept

The previous chapter revealed two motivational truths for leaders to consider. Now it's time to delve deeper into this conversation on human motivation—why people do what they do. I'll share three fundamental pieces of the motivational puzzle in the pages that follow. But I want to begin by sharing the foundation of that pattern. I refer to it as the cornerstone of human behavior or, simply, the cornerstone concept.

It asserts that *all human behavior is directed toward the satisfaction of needs.*

Here's a quick mental exercise for you. Review that 10-word phrase one more time, and see if you can determine the single most important word in it.

If you're like most people I ask, you're probably thinking it's *needs, satisfaction, behavior,* or *human,* in that order. But all those are wrong. You then might reexamine the phrase with furrowed brow, this time employing the process of elimination. Eventually, you would hesitantly ask whether *all* was that single most important word—and then you'd be right!

It's hard for some people to imagine that little three-letter word anchoring a concept as important and far-reaching as human motivation, but it does. The foundational cornerstone statement does not suggest that some or most human behavior is directed toward the satisfaction of needs. It literally says *all* human behavior is.

Now that's powerful. Think about it. *All* encompasses everything we do, say, or think, as well as what we don't do, don't say, or don't think. And all of our behavior is directed toward the conscious or subconscious attempt to satisfy some real or imagined need we have. That means literally everything you have done or will do today has been or will be ultimately directed toward the purpose of satisfying some need—in actuality, many needs.

Let's see if we can make this concept a bit more practical. Since I believe all human behavior is directed toward satisfying some need, I therefore believe you're engaging in this behavior—reading this book—to satisfy some need. An important concept relating to human behavior that *Leaders Ought to Know* and remember is this: A single action or behavior may result from many different needs. So for illustrative purposes, let's consider some needs that might drive you to read this book.

Maybe you're one of those folks with an insatiable hunger for any and all information related to leadership development and improvement.

Or maybe you're currently struggling with a specific leadership challenge, and you're attempting to research corrective techniques.

Of course, it's possible that your boss or professor designated this book as a professional or educational reading assignment.

And let's not overlook the fact that you might be a professional colleague, friend, or even family member of mine, and you're worried that my feelings might be hurt if you don't read this book.

Or though I like this possibility the least, maybe you're reading this book because your spouse left it on the bedside table and it looks to you like the perfect cure for insomnia.

Reading this book may help satisfy every single one of these needs.

There may very well be singular behaviors that individuals employ for the purpose of satisfying multiple needs.

Now let's consider another example of how needs can drive human behavior. But this time, instead of the same behavior resulting from many different needs, let's explore how one need may result in many different behaviors. Let's assume you have an employee who is motivated by money (his need). Now let's consider various alternatives that are available that might help him satisfy that need—depending on how badly he needs it.

If his need for money was not especially pressing:

He might participate in unpaid internships in hopes of having some future employer notice his skills and potential. He might commit to a multiyear trade apprentice program to learn valuable work skills, or he might return to college or trade school to further his educational development.

If his need for money was more immediate:

He might volunteer to work additional hours (overtime). He might moonlight, taking on a second or even third job. Or he might relocate in search of better-paying jobs in another geographic region.

If his need for money was immediate and critical:

He might borrow it. He might suck up to his boss (or others), begging for it. Or he might just steal it.

I think we can agree these are examples of very different behaviors, each directed toward satisfying the same need.

Now, here is a most important question. Review the list of these behaviors and ask yourself honestly if you can imagine yourself doing all the things listed just to get more money.

The vast majority of the people I ask this question say no. They can see themselves doing some but not all. Then I change the question slightly: "How many of you can imagine there is someone out there who would do all those things just to get more money?" Upon considering that question, almost every person I ask says yes.

I then pose the final question: What's the difference between you (who wouldn't do those things) and someone else (who might do those things)? Please don't say or think that you're more ethical or moral or you possess stronger values—because the real reason for the difference is far more fundamental than that.

The reason one person will do something that another person may choose not to do—or even refuse to do—is the level of need he or she is experiencing in that moment. That's why I advise people to never say *never*—as in "I would never do that job," "I would never let him talk to me that way," or "I would never stoop so low as to ask for help from her." The one thing that's certain is that you never know.

It's much better to say, "I would *prefer* to not have a need to do that job," "I would *hope* there would never be a need for him to talk to me that way," or "I *expect* that I'd never need to impose on her to get my work done."

What, Not Why

If you're still processing the cornerstone concept, that's fine. Take your time—because it's important, and you need to get it right. What you understand and come to grips with today is certain to be of great help to you for years to come in your ever-expanding leadership roles. Conversely, what you gloss over or take for granted today may continue to haunt you for years to come.

As for me, I'm all in. I embraced the cornerstone concept years ago, and it's never failed me. I have absolutely no doubt that all human behavior—what we see, as well as what we don't—is directed toward an individual's ultimate goal of satisfying existing needs.

When you finally reach that same conclusion, something amazing is bound to happen. You'll immediately be freed from the burden of a specific, nagging question that has troubled managers and supervisors, mothers and fathers, friends and neighbors, foreign leaders and diplomats, forever. The nagging question I'm referring to is the *why* question.

"*Why* did he say that?"

"*Why* won't she listen to me?"

"*Why* would he do exactly the opposite of what I suggested?"

"*Why* is she acting so selfishly?"

"*Why* won't he finish that report?"

"*Why* is she constantly late for work?"

The question of *why* has unlimited variations. But the amazing, freeing revelation associated with each is that once you accept and embrace the cornerstone concept, you never again have to ask the *why* questions relative to human behavior. Because at this point, we realize people are doing, saying, acting, delaying, coming, going, finishing, starting, speaking up, shutting down, and more, all for the express purpose of satisfying one or more needs that exist within them.

But in the absence of the *why* question, a far more important question takes center stage—the *what* question. Instead of asking why someone would do this or that, we instead should be asking, "*What* need would result in the behavior I'm witnessing?"

The important distinctions between these two questions shouldn't be missed or glossed over.

Why is a reactive question; *what* is a proactive question.

We ask *why* something happened after it has already occurred. We ask *what* is happening in advance of or during the occurrence.

We're constantly playing defense when asking *why*— trying to stop or repair something that is happening or has already happened. We're on the offense when we ask *what* because we're looking and moving forward and trying to make good things happen.

The differences in the two concepts are stark. Too many managers and supervisors are content to ask *why* and then complain that the answers they get are beyond their control. Proactive leaders ask *what* and then move forward expectantly, working alongside their followers to satisfy the individual needs they've identified.

Determining Individual Needs

Okay, it's time to take this needs identification a step further. It's not uncommon for someone to say to me, "Phil, I admit, this concept makes sense to me. But how can I actually determine my followers' individual needs?"

That's a fair question that deserves a logical, commonsense answer.

There are three primary ways to determine your followers' needs—and none works perfectly. But when applied in concert, each of the three has utility and benefit that can support the other two. The three ways are to ask, to observe, and to listen.

First, the *most obvious* way to determine someone's needs is to ask them.

"Ask and you shall receive; seek and you shall find; knock and the door shall be opened to you." Truth knows no timeline. The validity of asking, seeking, and knocking is as real today as when this truth was penned two millennia ago.

But asking alone is no surefire guarantee that you'll learn what you need to know about the needs driving your followers' behavior. Yes, some people readily share their needs when asked. They'll be thrilled you cared enough to inquire. However, don't be surprised if others respond to your question with little more than a blank stare and a mumbled "I don't know." Some needs are so deep-seated that it's difficult to understand them, much less verbalize them.

You should also know this: Some individuals may know very well what their needs are but still not share them with you if asked. They may choose to withhold such personal information out of fear and uncertainty as to how you'll use it. Until they feel completely comfortable that they can share their deepest needs with you without the risk of being hurt in any way, they'll hold back intentionally.

Second, the *best* way to determine someone's needs is to observe them.

In their groundbreaking book, *In Search of Excellence*, Tom Peters and Robert Waterman introduced the world to a commonsense technique they called MBWA—Management by Walking/Wandering Around. The premise was simple: Get out of your office and go where your followers do their work if you really want to get to know them and what their needs are.

For years, I've told managers and supervisors that conservatively (I actually believe it's significantly higher) at least 25 percent of their employees will never voluntarily come to the manager's or supervisor's office. They'll come if beckoned or required; otherwise, they'll simply stay in the work areas where they feel most comfortable. That means that you may never learn from or about them if you don't go to them.

The best way to determine an individual's needs is to watch and learn from them. However, if you've created a situation (either intentionally or unintentionally) in which you infrequently observe your followers, you really have no idea what their needs are. On those rare occasions when you do finally come around, they'll change their behavior (that is, clean up their act) until you leave, at which time they'll slip back into their more comfortable patterns of routine behavior. But you'll never know—because you're not there often enough to observe them when they don't take notice of your presence.

The more you walk or wander around, the better you'll know your followers and their needs. The less you do so, the less you know—and the more insulated you become from the needs that drive their behaviors.

Finally, the *worst* way to determine someone's needs is to listen solely to others as they talk about your followers and their needs.

Don't get me wrong. There is valuable information to be gained by actively listening to others. However, as it relates to identifying the needs of others, we cannot expect to learn a great deal about one person by simply listening to another. Any information we gain from a third party will always be tainted, even prejudiced (positively or negatively), by their past experiences or personal biases.

Unfortunately, this particular method is the one the lazier managers and supervisors among us employ most often. "John, what's going on with Bill?" or "Sally, tell me what you know about Suzanne's long-range plans."

There's nothing wrong with quizzing John or Sally and thus learning all that is possible from them about Bill and Suzanne. However, to stop there and not go further by talking directly with and observing Bill and Suzanne is simply unwise.

More often than not, employees are not fully motivated by the job they have so much as the needs that job is able to satisfy (e.g., challenge, creativity, security, recognition, growth). For leaders to create a self-motivating environment, they must get to know their employees' needs. But be warned: It's neither quick nor easy to do so. It requires a significant investment of time and energy, as well as a sincere interest in people. However, if you don't possess the sincere interest in people I'm referencing, do yourself and your followers a favor and move on to some other position (without people) that you can be sincere about.

Easiest or Shortest

My young son burst through the back door. He was dripping wet, having come straight from the swimming pool. Small puddles formed with every step he took. From where I was sitting, I could see his towel and shirt still lying outside on the pool deck.

"Joe," I said rather calmly, "go dry off and get your shirt on if you're coming in the house."

"I'm just going next door to play with Mallory," he said, as he continued his path across the family room, heading toward the door to the front yard.

"That's fine," I said, a bit more definitively, "but dry off and get your shirt on first."

"But, I'm just gonna be over there a minute," he countered as he kept moving across the room. By this time, his hand was on the doorknob.

"Hey!" I shouted. "I told you you're not going anywhere until you get dried off and get that shirt on."

Joe's forward motion stopped. Still grasping the doorknob, he turned to face me, before asking me the most curious question: "So, I have to dry off and get my shirt on before I go see Mallory, right?"

I looked at him and simply said, "That's right," at which point he immediately released the doorknob, spun around, and sprinted across the room, out the door, and to the pool deck. Once there, I watched as he scooped up his towel and shirt in one fluid motion, both drying off and putting his shirt on while at a dead run. When he reentered the room, he breathlessly asked, "It's okay for me to go see Mallory now?"

I said, "Go!" and he was gone.

I believe that little exchange illustrates the second piece of our motivational puzzle, which is that *people generally focus on and take the easiest route available to satisfy their needs.*

Notice I stress that people take the easiest route, not the shortest route. Some people may think my son was just being hardheaded when I had to repeat three times what I intended for him to do—and that thought crossed my mind initially as well. After all, he is his father's boy, and we all know that the apple doesn't fall too far from the tree.

However, after more thought and consideration—and asking myself specifically what need might've been driving Joe's behavior in that moment—I came to the following conclusion: Joe was not willfully trying to disobey me. Instead, he was just being driven by a most compelling need in that moment—the need to go see his friend Mallory.

Not once did he say to me that he didn't want to dry off or get his shirt on. That wasn't his focus. His focus was firmly fixed on getting to Mallory's as quickly and easily as possible. And from his single-minded perspective, the easiest way to satisfy that need was to run dripping wet and half-naked across our family room.

It wasn't until I exercised a bit of my parental authority (aka raising my voice) and thereby created a substantial hurdle to Joe's immediate plans that he actually had to stop and reconsider. When it became clear that he wasn't going anywhere until he met certain preliminary provisions (the towel and the shirt), he recalculated. He then determined that it would actually be quicker and easier to reverse field, run to get the towel and the shirt, and then dash on to Mallory's—rather

Why People Do What They Do

than stand and argue his case with this hardheaded old man (me). In this way, the new route he chose for satisfying his need once again became the easiest one.

And so it is with our followers.

For some of them, the easiest path to satisfying their needs may seem to be the path of least resistance—the one where they steer clear of obvious or perceived obstacles. Others may see the easiest route as straight ahead, bulldozing their way through any and all obstacles that might hinder their forward progress.

Why do different people perceive one route to be easier than another? Is it that one has significantly fewer obstacles or that one is simply more familiar—thus easier to negotiate— than another?

Almost everything we do in life is difficult when we're first learning to master the activity. But once mastered, it seems easier to keep doing it the same way rather than learn a new shortcut that might prove more beneficial.

Preparing for Unsatisfied Needs

The final piece of the puzzle that can help us understand why people do what they do is actually broken into three smaller pieces.

Let's face facts: Life is not perfect. Therefore, there's no way to satisfy every need that we or our followers have. Leaders need to be fully advised and aware that predictable behaviors will occur when a follower's needs are not being satisfied. Though I can't predict with certainty the order in which these behaviors will surface, you can anticipate three specific ones.

Behavior #1: When needs are not satisfied, some followers will withdraw.

Withdrawal comes in two general varieties: the most *obvious* form and the most *common* form. The most obvious form—physical withdrawal—simply means that your people quit and leave. They decide to voluntarily remove themselves from a situation that doesn't allow them the needs satisfaction they so desperately desire. They determine for themselves that it's best to search elsewhere to have their critical needs met. In other words, they've given up on you, their leader, being willing or able to help them.

The specific needs in question may vary as widely as your followers' personalities. However, many followers experience needs for trust, respect, attention, direction, opportunity, patience, feedback, support, understanding, consistency, recognition, praise, compassion, empathy, caring, and so on.

If employee retention or turnover rates in your organization or department aren't what you'd like them to be, it's well worth your time to investigate what employee needs are not being met that are ultimately driving people away. Exit interviews are one method that organizations have historically used to get honest feedback from departing employees. However, as honest as they may be in an exit interview, it's too little, too late for those employees. We've already lost them; they've decided to move on.

Proactive leaders recognize the need to talk with every one of their existing followers frequently—while they're still physically present—in an effort to determine individual needs and work closely with them when their needs aren't being met. If such communication between leader and follower is lacking, the stage is set for followers to possibly move toward the other—and more common—type of withdrawal.

This is a situation where your people quit . . . and stay. And this kind of emotional withdrawal can be far more devastating to an organization than physical withdrawal over the long haul.

Followers are still physically present when they withdraw emotionally; however, they're not mentally engaged. They go through the motions of their job every day but with no discernible commitment or passion for the organization, much less for the attainment of its goals and objectives. Productivity, morale, and teamwork suffer as employees wallow in the deepening quagmire of their own unsatisfied needs.

This is precisely why leaders must engage in intentional, ongoing interaction with all followers in an attempt to recognize their needs proactively. It's a task that they should neither overlook nor delegate—and one they must view as time invested, not time spent or wasted.

Behavior #2: When needs are not satisfied, some followers will become aggressive.

Some employees withdraw when faced with the reality of unsatisfied needs. However, others become ever more aggressive in their attitude and behavior. If a leader knows her followers well, it's not hard to recognize aggressive behavior in them.

Employees may balk when given certain work assignments. They may be quick to take exception to something someone said or did to them on the job, thus causing a seemingly unnecessary confrontation. Or the opposite may be true. Normally talkative, outspoken individuals may fall silent during discussions or interactions where their normal, expected input would be appropriate and valued.

How many times have you witnessed an employee behaving in a particular way and caught yourself wondering *What's gotten into him?* or *I've never seen her act that way before.*

If you witness a normally mild-mannered, subdued employee reacting in an unusually aggressive manner, don't be surprised when you find that they're not only venting their frustration but also fighting to have some specific need met. The best leaders realize that investing some focused, one-on-one time with that individual—in an effort to determine what specific need could be driving such drastic behavior—is ultimately time well spent. Working together, you and your follower may be able to determine positive, proactive steps designed specifically to address and resolve the problem.

I do need to highlight one of the more uncomfortable aspects of our leadership responsibilities at this point. I'm referring to leaders' need to be aware of and focused on the possibility of workplace violence. I readily admit that I'm not an expert on this topic. However, there is one thing I know and that every leader ought to recognize as well. If you witness the first signs of uncharacteristically aggressive behavior in the workplace, your observation demands your immediate attention before a situation gets out of hand.

The worst possible decision you can make in the face of uncharacteristically aggressive behavior is to ignore it in the feeble hope that it will simply go away. If your followers have become uncharacteristically aggressive for any reason, you can't predict what they will do next because they don't know themselves. As their leader, you should do no less than attempt to offer your follower help, guidance, and support during a difficult and troubling period for you both.

Remember, being a leader means there will be occasions when we have to step up and do the unpleasant things that others either can't or won't do. It's our professional and moral responsibility.

Behavior #3: When needs are not satisfied, some followers will rationalize.

The third predictable human response to the reality of unsatisfied needs is the act of rationalization. Your followers will attempt to rationalize away situations once they sense no other way to satisfy their existing needs.

The best lay definition of rationalization I've ever heard is this: "To rationalize is to tell 'rational lies.'"

I've never forgotten that. Think about it:

Rational: logical, reasonable, sensible, acceptable.

Lies: fabrications, deceptions, falsehoods, untruths.

When someone engages in rationalization, they're intentionally creating and telling themselves logical, acceptable untruths and then choosing to believe those self-created untruths and ultimately acting on them as if they were the truth. In other words, these people opt to create a fictionalized reality rather than search for real solutions to the challenges they face.

Emotional Defense Mechanisms

I distinctly remember the following encounter from a public seminar I was leading several years ago. I'd just finished discussing these three predictable responses to unsatisfied needs when one of the session participants spoke up.

"Mr. Van Hooser, I find this discussion quite intriguing," she offered. "You do realize that your discussion and explanation of people's predictable responses to their unsatisfied needs aligns itself perfectly with a psychological concept I share with clients in my clinical practice."

"No," I admitted, "I didn't realize that." I went on to admit to her and the assembled group that my formal knowledge of clinical psychology was quite limited.

"Well, your use of withdrawal, aggression, and rationalization as a predictive means of dealing with unsatisfied needs is what I and my professional colleagues would refer to as emotional defense mechanisms," she explained.

I'm pretty sure that was the first time I'd ever heard the phrase *defense mechanism* used in such a way. And as far as I could tell, it was totally appropriate. That's because people are always on the defensive when their needs are not being satisfied.

And it just so happens that if you take the three emotional defense mechanisms we've discussed and align them vertically, you would notice that the beginning letter of each spells out an interesting word: WAR.

Withdrawal

Aggression

Rationalization

I'm not a clinical psychologist, but even I know that when needs are not being satisfied, a psychological war is raging inside each of us. And in the midst of any type of conflict, we all want to be able to clearly identify both our enemies and our allies.

As a proactive leader, the quicker you identify yourself as an ally and not an enemy in your follower's personal WAR against unsatisfied needs, the quicker you will be able to move toward managing the negative effects of unsatisfied needs. It can be done. And I will show you how as we continue to explore together the nature of preventive leadership.

Chapter 8

Preventive Leadership

Ground Rule #8

Leaders don't overreact to problems;

Leaders prevent problems before they materialize.

Practicing PM

Auto mechanics advise automobile owners to change the oil in their vehicles every 3,000 to 5,000 miles. They know that doing so has proved effective in extending the functional life and performance of an automobile's engine—and therefore helps vehicle owners avoid unnecessary, costly, and untimely breakdowns, repairs, and replacements.

Heating and air conditioning professionals advise homeowners to change the filters in their units every one to three months. Why? Because doing so has proved effective in extending the functional performance of HVAC systems, thus allowing homeowners the opportunity to reduce or avoid unnecessary downtime, repairs, and higher energy costs.

Dentists advise patients to brush and floss daily and to schedule regular dental examinations every 6 to 12 months. Why? Because doing so has proved effective in extending the functional performance of teeth and gums, thus maintaining desirable oral health and avoiding unnecessary discomfort, ill health, and expense.

These examples are practical manifestations of a universally accepted concept that's commonly referred to as preventive maintenance (PM). When I ask workshop participants for a working definition of PM, I normally get the following: "It's the process of fixing something before it breaks."

The primary implication in this definition is that if left unattended, everything will eventually break (or break down). I agree completely. And most of us would also agree that once things start to go wrong, they can go terribly wrong, very quickly.

Remember Murphy's Law? Our old buddy Murphy advised us: If anything can go wrong, it will. Additionally, MacGillicuddy's Corollary to Murphy's Law holds that things that go wrong will do so at the most inopportune time! Therefore, common sense dictates that the prudent thing to do is to fix everything we can before, not when or after, it breaks.

Embracing PL

If it makes good common sense to practice PM (preventive maintenance) on vehicles and machinery, wouldn't it also make good common sense to provide preventive care for followers? I certainly think so. And I think we can do so proactively, in the form of what I like to call PL—preventive leadership.

My definition of PL is virtually the same as the definition offered for PM, with one important distinction. Instead of the focus being on something ("It's the process of fixing something before it breaks"), leaders need to be constantly concerned about someone ("It's the process of fixing someone before he or she breaks").

Experienced leaders know that having employees virtually guarantees that they'll eventually have employee problems—or breakdowns. They anticipate and prepare for them. They ready themselves. And as a result, they're not surprised when these problems happen.

They understand that employees don't just decide one day to become disconnected or dysfunctional in their work and professional attitudes. They recognize that professional breakdowns and employee failures usually happen over an extended period of time, for any number of reasons and in full view of those who should be paying attention—and who should be taking preventive action.

But let's make this more personal. Seldom will an employee walk into your office and quit her job without previously exhibiting preliminary signs of dissatisfaction, discontent, or frustration. As her leader, did you see it coming? Were you really listening to the complaints she voiced in the past? If yes, what specific actions did you take to help her satisfy the lacking needs driving her less-than-desirable behavior? Did you take any measures to prevent the ultimate dissolution of your professional relationship with her?

On the other hand, if you honestly didn't see it coming—then why not? What obstacles kept you from recognizing her professional annoyances? Were you paying appropriate attention? Did you let her know that you were available for conversation, encouragement, and even professional counseling? Are you willing to accept the proper measure of blame for the ultimate termination of this professional relationship?

Preventive leadership requires proactive leaders to con- sistently spend time with every follower whenever, wherever, and for as long as such opportunities exist. It's intended to provide an attentive approach via strategic thinking and focused questioning—a method that will help leaders under- stand their followers' specific needs before an unnecessary breakdown in the working relationship occurs.

Do Leaders Really Think?

During one of his easily forgettable movie roles, the late comic actor John Candy stared down from the movie screen and spoke words I've never forgotten. "I'm so highly educated," he pro- claimed proudly, "I don't even have to think before I speak."

This line was clearly written and delivered with the intent to entertain and make the audience laugh. Unfortunately, aspiring leaders also speak and make critical decisions without the benefit of careful thought and consideration far too often. And that usually proves to be anything but funny!

It pains me to say so, but it's increasingly rare to find a thinking leader in most organizations today. Why is that? Why don't leaders dedicate and assign time to thinking more? I believe it's because we leaders have casually allowed our- selves to become professional reactors—knee-jerk decision makers, if you will. Out of habit or necessity, leaders spend an inordinate amount of their time each day scurrying to and fro, hastily reacting to various situations and scenarios that arise on their watch.

Don't get me wrong: Reacting is not new, it's not always bad, and working this way is frequently necessary. But they must also be aware that this kind of reactive behavior is the antithesis of preventive leadership.

Preventive leadership is supported by focused thought and careful consideration of those things that might one day break a follower's will, desire, or commitment. If a leader can unearth such frequently hidden information—by thinking the right thoughts and asking the right questions—such a leader may take proactive measures to correct the problem before it becomes full-blown.

Six Thought Processes to Support Preventive Leadership

In essence, *Leaders Ought to Know* is more about PL, thinking proactively, and the good that can result from doing so. After all, there will never be a shortage of opportunities to think. Consider these six thought processes.

Explorative Thought—Asking Why?

The explorative thought form requires that leaders attempt to better understand their followers' needs while creating a rational, even predictable order to the environment around them. Explorative thought leaders take what others might casually consider random or commonplace occurrences and seek to apply their connectedness and interrelated rationale to future acts of team building, decision making, and problem solving.

Unfortunately, as valuable as it is, explorative thought is not nearly as common in the workplace as it should be. As twentieth-century financier and philanthropist Bernard Baruch once observed, "Millions saw the apple fall, but Newton was the one who asked why." This is precisely why leaders who take the time to ask why can stand out from the crowd, all the while discovering information of inestimable value.

Sample questions related to explorative thought include:

"Why did you settle on finance, over other business curriculum options, as your primary educational field of study?"

"Why are you now interested in moving away from the area of finance after attaining five years of practical experience in it, toward a new career in commercial real estate?"

Comparative Thought—Asking Why Not?

Leaders who employ the comparative thought approach take the why question to a higher, more advanced level. Melding what we've already come to know, understand, and accept with new information and advanced forward thinking allows the opportunity to compare what is already good with what might be even better. It's the same thought process that served candy makers well years ago, when they combined two individual snack favorites—chocolate and peanut butter—in a new form known as Reese's Cups. The result—a runaway candy best seller!

A why not leadership attitude doesn't just have the potential to produce a more creative work environment, it may also provide encouragement for continuous personal and professional growth and improvement, because it consistently challenges the established norm.

Examples related to comparative thought include:

"Why not assign Mervin, our most senior engineer, to mentor our newest engineer, Matthew, for the next six months? Matthew should realize the practical benefit from Mervin's extensive engineering background—and Mervin would have the opportunity to work directly with and learn from this 20-something."

"Why not expand our internal communication efforts by creating a weekly online town hall meeting format, featuring key employees each time? They could address current issues facing the organization and answer related questions in a direct and timely manner."

Predictive Thought—Asking When?

Predictive thought embraces a somewhat more scientific approach than the other two processes discussed so far. This approach requires leaders to collect and use analytical information, thereby enabling them to draw on such information for future projections, forecasts, even calculated predictions. It's not perfect science, of course, but if the analytical information on which this thought process is based is valid, leaders can make concrete plans as to when they should take or legitimately delay focused action.

Examples related to predictive thought include:

"When our new managerial trainee Beth completes the annual budget preparations, are there any other obstacles that would keep her from transitioning into the southeastern regional manager's position very quickly?"

"When Javier and his team finish installing the new packaging equipment, would he respond positively to the challenge of serving on the safety committee as they formulate revised safety procedures regarding that same equipment and its usage?"

Creative Thought—Asking What If?

The creative thought process can provide a stimulating mental environment; it stretches the boundaries of our own creativity and imagination as we continue to search for yet undiscovered possibilities and opportunities. What-if questions are most effective when presented in a nonthreatening environment, where no commitment to do anything is immediately required—thus making anything possible. What-if questions are most powerful when presented with a positive tone. This kind of creative thought can provide a welcome break from the monotony of our normal reactionary tendencies.

Examples related to creative thought include:

"What if we required all of our cost accountants to spend at least a month working as inspectors who monitor inventory control? Would that help Brenda and Wally become more aware of and responsive to the needs of that department's employees?"

"What if we allowed all our sales team unrestricted travel opportunities—let them go on-site to visit customers whenever the customer requested, without requiring managerial approval? Would that be helpful in building stronger client relationships?"

Deliberative Thought—Asking How?

Here beats the heart of rational thought and deliberation for pragmatic leaders everywhere. Let's face it: Attempting to act on every what-if question wouldn't lead to consistently prudent leadership decisions. The truth is that some ideas are good, and some simply aren't—and leaders need a practical way to distinguish between the two. This is what makes the how question so important for leaders. It allows us to create and communicate a defined order to our world. Even the most creative, flamboyant, reactive leaders need to be held accountable for the how of any commonsense, foundational thought process.

Examples related to deliberative thought include:

"How can we create a system that would allow Juanita the freedom to approve customer requests immediately and still communicate those decisions to other affected team members in a timely fashion?"

"How can we involve Patricia in the design and rollout phases of the new product lineup, without having Rachel assume that we no longer value her input?"

Interactive Thought—Asking What Do You Think?

The most successful, proactive leaders immediately recognize this question's intrinsic value. Unfortunately, few traditional managers do. Taking the time and making the effort to ask followers what they truly think—with a genuine desire to know the answers—mentally and emotionally engages both individuals and teams. And effective leaders must know what to do after asking the question: They must sit down, shut up, and listen actively. The freedom to share what we actually think, without fear of correction, rebuttal, or reprisal, is a powerful motivational force for followers everywhere. To stifle or disallow such freedom can have a withering effect on both the short- and long-term working relationship between leaders and followers. But when managed properly, interactive thought propels even ordinary individuals toward extraordinary effort and accomplishments.

Questions related to interactive thought include:

"Jackie, what do you think we should do to improve new face boss orientation and training efforts for the number 9 mine?"

"Mia, what do you think we should offer employees who are required to relocate to new company assignments in new international locations?"

"I'm Moving to Alaska!"

Of course, there will be times while you're striving to be a preventive leader that you won't have the luxury of thinking progressive thoughts and planning proactive questions. Sometimes our followers prove themselves—through their unanticipated actions—to be more proactive than their leaders.

It was a beautiful Sunday afternoon in Florida. While my family enjoyed time outdoors, I caught up on overdue paperwork in my office. Then the phone rang.

"Hello?"

"Hi, Phil, this is Stacy."

Identifying herself was mere courtesy. I recognized her voice immediately. Stacy was my accountant. She'd managed the bookkeeping and income tax preparation functions for my business and personal accounts for several years. We talked regularly. However, I was pretty sure we'd never before talked on a Sunday.

"Stacy, I wasn't expecting to hear from you today. Is everything all right?" I asked.

"Yeah, Phil, everything's fine. I've been meaning to call you for a couple of weeks now, but I didn't want to interrupt you during office hours. I knew you worked weekends sometimes. I'm glad I caught you. Is now a good time to talk?"

My curiosity was piqued. Stacy sounded relaxed, but I could still sense a note of anxiety in her voice.

"Sure, Stacy. What's on your mind?"

"Phil, what can you tell me about corporate accounting? I know you're not an accountant, but you've spent a lot of time working in corporate environments and I value your opinion, so I thought I'd ask."

My curiosity was now on full alert. I cautiously began offering a broad review of what little I knew to be the responsibilities of a corporate accountant as compared with those of a public accountant. But all the while, I kept wondering where her question was coming from. I had to ask.

"Well, Stacy, I know it's not much, but now you know all I know about corporate accounting. But now it's my turn. I've got a question for you. What's really going on here?"

Stacy chuckled.

"Well, I figured you'd ask, and I'm okay with telling you. But please don't mention any of this to my boss. You know

167

Preventive Leadership

Fred; he'd go crazy if he thought I was even thinking about making a change. I like my job; I really do. But I'm concerned. My career has basically stalled, and I don't know what Fred or the other partners have in mind for me in the future. Unfortunately, I don't think Fred is even aware of my concern. If he is, he certainly hasn't said anything. While it'd be great if he initiated the conversation, I'm sure he won't. And I'm afraid if I had this conversation with him that he'd overreact, big time. Who knows? He might even fire me on the spot. And I just can't risk that, Phil. I need a job. But I also need some help and guidance. I was thinking about people I respect and trust. That's why I called you."

Stacy was a divorced, single mother of a young son. She went into greater detail explaining her current professional and financial challenges. She explained that her divorce had forced her to drop out of college a year short of finishing her accounting degree. Initially, her practical skills and general education were sufficient to land a basic bookkeeping job with the firm. She had accepted her current job several years before as a basic means of providing for herself and her son. However, despite her capabilities and years of experience, she wasn't eligible to sit for the CPA exam unless she had an accounting degree. This also meant that she had virtually no upward mobility within her current firm or any other. As the years rolled by, she was becoming ever more aware of the growing financial pressures that awaited her as her son got older.

Stacy admitted to me that she loved public accounting, but she would have to seriously consider moving to the corporate side if the money was good enough. She ended her explanation by asking me one more question, and it was a particularly tough one: She wanted to know what I thought she should do.

"Stacy, believe me, I want the best for you and your son, whatever that might be. At the same time, I must admit that I'd hate to see you leave public accounting. You're the primary reason I still do business with your firm. You have a special talent for interacting with your clients."

"Stacy," I continued, "I'm not going to try to tell you what you should do; that's your call. But since you asked my opinion, I've got another question for you."

"What is it, Phil?"

"Stacy, I hope you can be honest with yourself. Are you running from—or to—something?"

A long, pregnant silence followed my question. Finally, she spoke. "Yeah, well Phil, that's a great question. I've got to go now. Thanks."

With that said and nothing more, Stacy hung up. Just like that—abruptly. I seriously thought I might've upset her, but I didn't know how. I decided to let the matter rest for a few days.

Since I still hadn't heard back from Stacy after more than a week, I decided to give her a call.

"Hey, Stacy. Phil here."

"Hi, Phil. I'm glad you called. I've actually been meaning to call you to share my good news," she offered enthusiastically.

"Yeah? What good news is that?" I countered.

"In case you haven't heard, I'm moving to Alaska!"

Her announcement caught me completely by surprise. I could tell she wasn't joking.

"No, I hadn't heard. And I must admit, I didn't see that coming!" I said. "You're going to have to catch me up."

Preventive Leadership

Stacy immediately launched into a full explanation. I soon learned that Stacy was involved in a long-distance relationship with a guy from—guess where—Alaska. He had family in Florida, and he'd been making semiregular visits there to visit family and Stacy for the past year. Apparently, Stacy's beau was ready to take their relationship to the next level—marriage. Stacy, on the other hand, admitted that while she cared for the guy, she wasn't sure if she was ready for that level of commitment.

She explained that she'd casually been exploring professional and educational options in Alaska for the past few months. She'd intensified her efforts over the past several days and had discovered that her years of practical accounting experience made her eligible for scholarship monies and financial assistance at one of Alaska's public universities. In addition, an Alaskan contact had just offered Stacy a part-time job helping people file their income taxes. From her perspective, the pieces of the puzzle were coming together.

And it was all happening without Fred knowing anything about it.

"Phil, I should be able to finish my accounting degree and sit for the CPA exam within 18 months. I can do the job preparing taxes in my spare time, and it will cover my living expenses. During the next year and a half, my son will be able to experience a new culture before he gets to high school, and I'll be able to see if I really want to spend the rest of my life with this guy as my husband. So thanks, Phil. Your question was a good one. It made me think and helped me choose what I really wanted to do in the future."

Running from or to—and Why It's Important

Stacy's dilemma is relatively common among followers and leaders alike. When wrestling with unsatisfied personal or professional needs, our biggest struggle often is the one that originates in our minds.

Stacy admittedly was hesitant to approach her boss with her concerns. She had already determined in her head how Fred would respond if she did so. However, without his input, Stacy was left wondering what options were available that would allow her to remove herself from her current circumstance. She became convinced that moving 5,000 miles away was the only prudent action to take.

And maybe it was. However, I'm convinced that if Fred had practiced preventive leadership with Stacy over the years—by asking her well-developed questions and determining what she ultimately wanted to do with her career— things might've turned out differently. Stacy likely would have opened up long before she wanted to leave, and together they could've worked to avoid the ultimate professional breakdown (resignation) that resulted.

Do you remember the Three Stooges comedy shorts from years gone by? As a kid, I loved watching the slapstick skits and the ridiculous situations those Stooges got into. Though far from highbrow comedy, the antics of the Three Stooges (of which there were actually six over the years) made me laugh as a child and still make me smile.

Without question, my favorite Stooge was Curly. You remember Curly, don't you?

"Why, soitenly!" I can hear you saying. "He was the poifect Stooge!" Nyuk! Nyuk! Nyuk!

Okay, no more of that. I promise. But I believe one of the Three Stooges skits featuring Curly is valuable for leaders. Really! Let me set the scene.

Curly is alone in a room. He stands ready to open a door, behind which, unbeknownst to him, awaits a ferocious gorilla (or at least a man dressed in a gorilla costume wishing to appear ferocious). As he opens the door, the gorilla lunges forward, startling Curly. After employing that trademark Curly jump and shuffle, with three or four Curly "woop, woop, woops" thrown in for good measure, Curly darts away. Of course, while running forward—yet looking backward—Curly runs directly into the wall ahead of him. He is temporarily knocked senseless—and all of America laughed. Or at least, I did.

If you'll allow me, I'd like to dissect this little scenario to reveal three preventive leadership lessons. Consider the following questions and answers:

Q: What was Curly's immediate motivation when the gorilla leaped toward him?

A: To put distance between himself and the gorilla—as quickly as possible.

Q: What did Curly choose to do to make sure that he was actually escaping the perceived danger?

A: He attempted to run away, yet he continued to look back (at the gorilla) to see whether he was actually making progress.

Q: In so doing, what was the result for Curly?

A: Every obstacle that might've littered his path (including the wall), presented an unseen, unanticipated obstacle—risk—that he didn't notice, again because he was looking backward, not forward.

You see, Curly's ultimate plight was unsurprising for people like you and me who know to focus on the practical, predictable aspects of preventive leadership. However, Curly made the same mistake many uninformed leaders with unsatisfied needs make. He tried to escape something unpleasant, something he didn't welcome or enjoy, without a clear objective in mind as to where he was actually going, what he hoped to accomplish in the process, and what might stand in his way.

In the Old Testament Book of Proverbs, wise King Solomon warned, "Where there is no vision, the people perish" (Proverbs 29:18). In his mega-best-selling book, *The 7 Habits of Highly Effective People,* the late Stephen Covey reminded those of us who wish to live successful, fulfilled lives that we should "begin with the end in mind." Even the old western Kentucky farmers I encountered as a young boy seemed to embrace the same truth. "If you don't know where you're going, son," they cautioned, "any road will take you there—but you won't know when you get there 'cause you never really intended to be there in the first place."

The truth is the truth yesterday, today, and forever. Too many leaders and followers are simply running from something (a demanding boss, a stressful work environment, increasing workload, heightened professional expectations, a challenging economy—to name just a few). As they attempt to escape whatever they fear, they attempt to move forward, but

173

Preventive Leadership

they can't resist looking back. Why? Because their primary goal is to get away from something they don't like. As a result, they take very little time to evaluate the very real obstacles that might be before them—and therefore become immediately vulnerable to those obstacles.

And by the way, those obstacles are no respecters of persons. They have always been there and always will be. They don't change to ensnare one leader or one follower over another. No, the obstacles are always present—to everyone.

Yet, while some predictably fall victim to the obstacles, others ably maneuver their way through, over, and around those same obstacles—because these are the people who are looking and moving forward, not backward. The most successful leaders and followers are purposefully running to something, not from something. And leaders are most successful when they are able to help their followers do the same.

The Wisdom of Dumb Questions

As I mentioned earlier, I believe preventive leadership is based on the strength of strategic thinking—such as that discussed in the six thought processes—and wisdom is embedded in proactive questioning. The way we think is the way we act. Proverbs 23:7 says that "As a man thinketh in his heart, so is he." An Omaha Proverb says: "Ask questions from your heart, and you will be answered from the heart."

Throughout his professional life, the late management guru Peter Drucker encouraged managers to ask—and answer—his five management questions:

1. What is our mission?

2. Who is our customer?

3. What does the customer value?

4. What are our results?

5. What is our plan?

Drucker's clear-eyed approach to formulating questions that strike at the heart of what managers should know and do inspired me in the early part of my professional career. In more recent years, other thought processes have opened my mind to the practical, commonsense side of preventive leadership.

A few years back, I stumbled on an article by Geoffrey Colvin with an intriguing title: "The Wisdom of Dumb Questions" (*Fortune Magazine,* June 25, 2005, p. 157). Colvin surmised in the article that "dumb questions lead to smart decisions" and that a dumb question can "cut to the heart of the matter, posing a blunt challenge to someone or something—an authority, a policy, the established order."

Combining Drucker's penchant for asking probing questions that make managers think, with Colvin's observation that even a dumb question can cut to the heart of an important matter, I set about creating a list of questions that smart, proactive leaders should be asking their followers. I believe the answers to these questions may create an environment in which preventive leadership can take root and flourish.

Dumb Question #1: How Am I Doing?

This question was made popular by former three-term New York City Mayor Ed Koch. During his term as mayor (1978–1989), Koch was renowned for stopping average New Yorkers on the street and asking them this, his favorite dumb question. Why would he do such a thing? It's likely that he realized how easy it is for leaders to allow themselves to become isolated, even insulated from the followers they are entrusted to lead. If he didn't ask the common Joes and Janes, his only alternative would be to trust the opinions of his advisors—most of whom were even further removed from the man and woman on the street.

Dumb Question #2: What Have I Screwed Up Lately?

All of us enjoy having rose petals strewn before us. In other words, we like to hear people bragging and commenting on all the great things we have done and are doing. But the fact is those kinds of accolades really don't teach us very much. While praise is great for ego boosting, it's worthless when it comes to building a foundation for respect, trust, and continual improvement. Mistakes, errors, miscalculations, screwups—those are the things that can really teach us something. Think about it. Haven't you learned more from your mistakes over the years than from your successes? Well, then, why not spend some focused time seeking out areas where we seem to be chronically screwing up, in order to shine a bright light on those areas as we begin to proactively repair them?

Dumb Question #3: What Should I Be Doing Better?

Maybe you really are doing a great job, and people are honestly struggling to find concrete answers to your dumb question #2. Congratulations! You must be doing something right as a leader. Keep it up. But never forget that some sage once opined that "good is the enemy of great." And so it is. There's always room for improvement, and personal leadership improvement should be our never-ending quest—to be great at what we do and how we lead. Therefore, go out and ask your constituencies (the followers, customers, colleagues, partners that make up your professional existence) what they would like to see done better, sooner, at a more sophisticated level. Their answers may prove to shake the comfort zones you have unconsciously allowed to form around you. But they may also serve as the catalysts and personal motivation necessary to move you forward toward heightened levels of preventive leadership performance.

Dumb Question #4: What Would You Like Me to Do about That?

Some may categorize this as the dumbest question of all—and therefore the smartest one you can ask. Everyone has an opinion. And even the lowliest of employees are known to openly and freely share those opinions with everyone they encounter—fellow workers, family members, neighbors, even innocent bystanders waiting patiently in the grocery store checkout line—that is, with everyone but the person who needs to know most: you, their leader. Possibly the smartest thing a leader can do is to actively seek out other people's personal, specific opinions. Don't be afraid to ask them dumb question #4. And when you do, shut up and listen attentively. You'll find that what people might tell you—in astonishing detail—is nothing short of amazing, if you just ask. The chances are stacked heavily in your favor that you might just learn something from the conversation.

Now, I know what you're thinking—what about the worst-case scenario? What if they share unrealistic, unworkable, and practically impossible suggestions? What then? Don't worry; my advice is that you tell them just that. In an honest, open manner, of course, let them know what won't work *and,* most important, why. Most of us work with fairly reasonable people. If their suggestions are not feasible, based on your complete explanation, they'll understand. And even those who just refuse to understand can never claim you didn't make the effort to explain things to them.

How It's Done

Now that we've covered four good dumb questions that any leader can ask, maybe I should tell you how it's done best.

1. Don't label your question as a dumb one before you ask it. The fact that you have the courage to ask the obvious questions may actually make you look brilliant in others' eyes. Hey, it worked for Socrates. Remember the dumb question he asked: "What is virtue?" People thought that question was pretty smart.

2. Don't apologize for asking the question. Don't dilly-dally or tiptoe around the question until its lost its power and its oomph. Just step up and ask it—with sincerity and an open mind.

3. Don't worry about what the answer might be. You can't predict or control the future—not yours and certainly not someone else's. The answer will be what it is. You can begin to deal with it once it is revealed.

4. Don't be intimidated if people don't immediately offer a response. Be patient. Let them process the question appropriately. After all, this may be the very first time their leader ever asked them a dumb question—on purpose, at least.

Asking questions requires even the best leaders to move past their fears. In the next chapter, you will learn how to do just that.

Chapter 9

Fearsome Facts

Ground Rule #9

Leaders aren't fearless;

Leaders face their fears courageously.

Who's Your Daddy?

Two male friends and I had traveled from our homes in Missouri, Kentucky, and Virginia to Steamboat Springs, Colorado, for a weeklong snow-skiing vacation. I had skied before, but I was by no means an expert at the sport. Though my pride wouldn't allow me to admit it at the time, I was, in fact, the least experienced skier of our group. Nevertheless, we were all buoyed by a heaping helping of 20-something male machismo. Our inflated opinion of our own physical strength, courage, and overall alpine capabilities was in direct proportion to the testosterone coursing through our veins. And regardless of whether it was justifiable, we were supremely confident in our

181

individual abilities to handle whatever challenges the mountain presented us. Ready or not, here we came.

We spent Day One of our skiing adventure securing equipment, acclimating to the altitude, and getting a feel for the lower mountain. The weather was gorgeous, the scenery spectacular, and the ski runs expertly groomed. Everything was in alignment for a perfect ski vacation.

We skied a few beginner green runs on that first day to loosen up, several more advanced blue runs to push ourselves a bit, and even one or two of the moderately steep, but otherwise easily negotiable, lower mountain expert black runs just for bragging purposes. By the time the sun began to dip behind the western mountains, our confidence was as high as the Rocky Mountain sky.

For the remainder of the evening, we concentrated on reliving the day's runs and reviewing trail maps in anticipation of Day Two. Our plan of attack was simple. We'd be the first in line for the first ski lift of the day, bound for the mountain's peak. From there, we would ski nothing but blue and black runs all the way to the base of the mountain. The plan was a good one in concept. I was sure it would be an unforgettable experience.

In just a few hours, I'd be proven right.

We awoke to a classic Rocky Mountain snowstorm. A weather front had settled in during the night and was dumping a heavy accumulation of that champagne powder for which Steamboat Springs is known worldwide. Skiing powder is a real treat for expert skiers. But as mentioned previously, I was far from expert—and I'd never skied powder before. I was more familiar and comfortable with groomed slopes. The mere thought of skiing fresh snow, knee- to waist-deep, was not a comforting one for me. For the first time, I felt a slight gnawing fear develop deep in the pit of my stomach.

As the three of us loaded onto the mainline ski lift for the approximately nine-minute ride to the mountain's peak, I noticed that the view was starkly different from the day before. The wind was calm, but the air was thick with millions of huge snowflakes, each approximately the size of a quarter and falling gently, quietly, unobstructed to the ground. The flakes were so concentrated they created a literal whiteout, providing visibility of eight feet at best. As the lift carried us to the mountain's top, I saw nothing but snow above me, beneath me, all around me. It was as if I was floating, suspended in a sea of white. And I didn't especially like the feeling. It took me out of my comfort zone. That gnawing fear began to grow.

"Guys, let's bear to the left when we exit the lift."

The familiar voice broke the silence of the moment. It was Sean's, one of my traveling companions and the best skier of the bunch.

"If I remember right, there's either a blue or black run just to the left of the lift," Sean said before adding, "Just follow me."

I was already on high alert.

If I remember right? Well, which is it—blue or black? It makes a big difference to me right now. I know I can't see anything, and neither can you. We've never been this way before. Why should we follow you? Personally, I think we should talk about it more. It would be smarter if we took our time and looked around for awhile until we found a safer route down. Maybe a green run would be a better option.

These and other fear-driven thoughts flooded my consciousness. My bravado from the day before was nowhere to

Fearsome Facts

be found. Nevertheless, I suffered in silence, choosing to focus more on my fears—the unfamiliar terrain, the restricted visibility, my lack of confidence, the multitude of unknowns that lay ahead—than on what I might do to control them. As we drew ever closer to the mountain's peak, my anxiety threatened to overwhelm me; in fact, it bordered on debilitating. I was terribly afraid—and what was even *worse* was that I was afraid to let the others know that I was afraid. I simply wouldn't admit my fears publicly. Instead, I tried to fake it.

"Guys, why don't we just take a few minutes once we get to the top to determine exactly what our plan is?" I suggested meekly.

"No need," was Sean's steady, confident reply. "Don't worry, Phil, just follow me. I know where we are, and I know where we're going. If you need me, I'll be there."

At that moment, the lift reached the crest of the mountain—and I knew that the time for action had come. I had no other option. As our skis once again touched terra firma, with a little nudge from the lift's seat, aided by gravity, we skied forward, down a slight incline away from the lift.

I looked up just as my buddies pulled in front of me. Though it was hard to see from a distance, the grade ahead appeared to be significantly steeper. But my focus wasn't fixed on the grade; it was fixed on my friends—because the last thing I wanted was to lose sight of them. Though he was barely two body lengths ahead of me, it was already difficult to make out Sean's profile through the heavy snowfall. I locked my eyes on him (and unfortunately, not on my path), following dutifully as he made a hard left turn before disappearing suddenly from view.

An immediate sense of panic washed over me. I could no longer see Sean. He was gone. Desperately afraid of being left behind, I instinctively buried my ski poles deep in the snow ahead of me and gave a mighty pull. The effort caused me to lurch forward uncomfortably. Suddenly, without warning, I felt the tips of my skis leave the trail and drop over the edge of a previously unseen mountain ledge. In that instant, I caught a glimpse of the trail sign posted on the ledge above me. Unwittingly and unwillingly, I was now committed to a *double* black diamond run, featuring drastic elevation changes (it was very steep), moguls (it had frequent bumps), and natural environmental hazards (it was littered with boulders and trees).

My speed increased instantly and dramatically. Due to the extreme drop, I figure I descended 40 or 50 feet down the mountainside in no more than two seconds. It was terrifying. I didn't have time to think. I certainly didn't realize that I'd just become a living object lesson illustrating both the validity and the practicality of Sir Isaac Newton's Three Laws of Motion.

Newton's First Law

- An object at rest tends to stay at rest, and an object in motion tends to stay in motion, with the same direction and speed.

Newton's Second Law

- The acceleration of an object produced by a net (total) applied force is directly related to the magnitude of the force.

Newton's Third Law

- For every action (force) there is an equal and opposite reaction (force).

Had I paid more attention in science class years before, maybe I would've known what to do to avoid the collision course on which I found myself. But I hadn't—and apparently Newton's scientific principles had not been repealed for the purpose of assuring my personal safety. I was in motion and staying in motion, my acceleration had magnified, and I was getting more and more concerned about that action-reaction thing.

Try as I might, I couldn't stop under such conditions. For the next 200 or 300 yards, I was on my own little carnival ride—upright (temporarily), speed increasing, weaving precariously back and forth across the fall line—knowing all the while that I was desperately out of control but incapable of doing anything to proactively manage my situation.

I was moving, but I had no idea where I was going. I could see no further ahead than my current position. And though I wasn't comfortable where I was, I feared where I was going could be significantly worse. You might say, physically and psychologically, I was in deep, well, . . . powder.

And then, just as quickly as it began, it all came undone.

My left ski tip struck a hidden obstacle buried beneath the snow, causing both skis to separate. Due to my speed and inexperience, I was unable to maintain my balance and regain control. As I heaved forward, falling headfirst down the mountain, my right ski separated from my ski boot and shot down the slope ahead of me. I did a face-plant in the fresh snow, careening and sliding downhill for another 15 or

20 yards before coming to rest, sprawled with my back against an exposed boulder.

I lay still for a long moment, taking inventory. My legs and arms still worked. I could still think and see—barely. There was no obvious puddle of blood in the snow. From all initial indications, I had escaped serious injury.

Another stroke of good luck was that my second ski and my ski poles were still in my possession. How we stayed together through the crash is still a mystery. In spite of these few things for which I was immediately thankful, new fears entered the picture.

Along with my ski, I'd lost my skiing buddies who I figured were certainly far down the mountain ahead of me by that point. There was no conceivable way they could climb back up to me, given the extreme terrain—even if they knew I needed their help. There were no other skiers in the area. Not another soul in sight. It was just me. I was all alone.

The thought of isolation was made more frightening by the reality that accompanied it. I quickly realized if I was to get down that mountain, it was going to be up to me alone to make it happen. Afraid or not, I couldn't stay up here forever. I had to face my fear—and then get to work in spite of it.

The steep slope made it necessary for me to scoot down the hill slowly, on my backside, all the while scanning the area with my eyes in search of my wayward ski. After moving about 15 to 20 feet downhill, I noticed its tip protruding from a snowbank. I made my way over to collect it and then, with considerable effort, managed to reattach it to my ski boot. Finally, several minutes after my unplanned separation from my buddies, I stood alone on the mountainside, bruised but

Fearsome Facts

not beaten, with approximately a mile and a half of rugged alpine terrain between me and the base.

As I caught my breath, I felt a final wave of fear begin to build. But the situation was different this time. This time I recognized the fear for what it was, and I began to dismiss it from my mind almost immediately. You see, I'd already decided that fearful or not, I had no choice but to face my situation head-on. In addition, I'd already begun to realize that despite the previous challenges, I had, in fact, survived all the things that had been frightening to me in the minutes before.

As pitiful as my feeble skiing attempts had been, I was still alive and in one piece—and that was success. In my case, failure had not been fatal. Yes, I'd failed to plan well. Yes, I'd failed to admit my inexperience and inadequacies to those who could've helped and supported me. Yes, I'd thought more highly of myself and my abilities than appropriate. Yet, despite it all, I was still standing—and I still had choices available.

Though now destined to do it alone, I was beginning to realize that I could do it—a thought that was both encouraging and energizing. My fear began to dissipate in that very moment—replaced by an utterly random thought.

For some odd reason that defies explanation still, as I stood on that mountainside, preparing for my deliberate descent, my mind reverted back to a favorite television series from my childhood. I found myself thinking about a 1950s–1960s era western drama called *The Rifleman*.

The show was about a widower father, Lucas McCain, who happened to be pretty handy with that nifty, customized rifle of his. The back story had Lucas raising a young son, Mark, as he grew toward manhood and independence, in a rather rugged, hostile environment on an isolated ranch located somewhere in the New Mexico territory during the 1880s.

As my attention left the mountain temporarily and turned to thoughts of the shoot-'em-up wild West portrayed in *The Rifleman,* an even more specific scene formed in my consciousness. I could see young Mark McCain, stranded, frightened, all alone, battling the natural elements in the midst of a howling blizzard. Terrified, panicked, and in great despair—trying to determine what to do next—I saw Mark in my mind's eye crying out in desperation—for the one he depended on most for help, guidance, and deliverance.

"Pa! Pa! Where are you, Pa?"

Isolated in the muffled silence of the mountainside, with the only discernible sounds my own labored breathing and heart beating, I found myself entertaining a ridiculous thought. I was actually considering whether to do it. Momentarily captivated by the unexplained memory of a long-since canceled television show, I wondered if it was a good idea.

Why not? What could it hurt? I asked myself. *Nobody will ever know.*

So, convinced that it was the thing to do at that moment in time, I cut loose!

"Pa! Pa!" I cried out loudly, "Where are you, Pa?"

Instantly, another voice sounded in response. The voice was familiar, emanating from an unseen, snow-shrouded location slightly farther down the mountain.

"Phil? Is that you?" I heard Sean call back. "Who are you yelling for? Who's 'Pa'?"

That's right. My friend and leader, Sean, had not continued down the mountain after all. He hadn't abandoned me. Like any

Fearsome Facts

good leader, he wouldn't leave his follower stranded, unaccounted for. He'd been there, waiting patiently for me, all along.

Followers appreciate leaders who have earned their respect, trust, and confidence over time. But I stress that such reverence is never given; it's always earned. Because Sean did not leave me this time, I would never have to wonder if he would leave me at some other time. He had my back. His past performance would offer me great confidence for the future. And so it is in the workplace. Followers determine what their leaders will do and how they will act in the future by what they've done and how they've acted in the past.

Somewhat embarrassed, but at the same time recognizing the absurdity and hilarity of the unexpected turn of events, my sense of humor resurfaced. I shouted back: "Of course that's not me! That's some idiot up here who can't ski a lick, calling for his daddy!"

I laughed out loud as I made my way slowly and deliberately to where Sean was waiting. Together, we continued down the mountain. My initial fears were long gone, replaced by a surging sense of commitment, accomplishment, confidence, and camaraderie.

Understanding Fears

Over time, many highly accomplished leaders have both acknowledged the significance of fear and trumpeted the importance of addressing it directly as something we must reckon with, beat back, and overcome.

As U.S. President Franklin D. Roosevelt famously proclaimed during his first presidential inaugural address, "The only thing we have to fear is fear itself." These words, spoken in 1933, were intended as encouragement and inspiration for a fearful nation reeling from the devastating financial and emotional calamities brought on by the Great Depression.

English poet and author of *The Hobbit* and *Lord of the Rings,* J. R. R. Tolkien wrote in *The Children of Húrin,* "The man that flies from his fear may find he has only taken a shortcut to meet it."

Have you ever attempted to avoid or escape from something that has or is producing fear in your life, only to encounter that very thing at some later juncture? The wise among us realize that while we may be able to run temporarily, we can never hide from the realities and responsibilities of the personal or professional leadership positions we occupy.

Consider the leader who fears confrontation and thus constantly strives to avoid it. Unbeknownst to him, this individual is destined to be confounded and consumed by various forms of confrontation going forward, because he never learned to manage those he was bound to encounter.

Or how about the leader who fails to act on what she knows she must do, for fear of having her detractors criticize her decision? Ironically, her hesitancy to act leads to the very thing she was hoping to avoid. Because she wouldn't act at all, she is ultimately condemned more broadly and soundly than she would've been, had she acted decisively in the first place.

One of my favorite quotes about fear is attributed to the first female Nobel Prize winner (1903, Physics). Marie Curie was a Polish physicist and chemist, whose pioneering work in the use of radioactivity led to significant breakthroughs in medical research still benefiting humankind today.

"Nothing in life is to be feared, it is only to be understood," she declared. "Now is the time to understand more, so that we may fear less."

The more we understand about the expectations heaped on us as leaders—expectations involving, for instance, enhanced performance, innovation, and employee engagement—the less we have to fear and the more intently we can address these expectations quickly and directly.

Therefore, in an effort to expose the commonsense realities associated with fear, I've isolated three fearsome facts worthy of a leader's consideration.

Fearsome Fact #1: We All Have Them

First of all, stop pretending that you're fearless. Not only is it disingenuous; according to some smart folks, it's also humanly impossible.

I read somewhere many years ago (the source long since forgotten) that every healthy human baby is born with two fears—and only two. Now, I wouldn't know how to validate that assertion; maybe no one can. Nevertheless, valid or not, that little-known tidbit has stuck with me. It's served me well as both a fun activity and a good interactive training exercise. I've asked various people to offer guesses regarding those two fears and have collected a variety of responses in return: starving, abandonment, facial hair, men, animals, clowns, heat, cold, dolls—and the list goes on. I'm sure there's some measure of logic in each answer (though I'm not willing to dig deep enough to uncover it).

But those two fears I remember being cited years ago made perfect sense to me then—and they still do now: the fear of falling and loud noises. Though a baby's motor skills and balance are still months, even years away from being fully developed, it's not unusual for a baby who's even just a few hours old to attempt to shift her little body if she feels as if she might be falling. Why would she do that? It's certainly not a learned behavior; remember, she's only hours old.

We can ask the same questions regarding a baby's response to loud noises. We realize that newborns are easily startled and will jump, sometimes even cry, at the sound of a loud, frightening noise. Again, how do they know to do that? No one has to teach them that behavior; it seems to be inborn.

Even if you disagree completely with the two inborn fears assertion, one thing you can't dispute is that most of the fears with which we struggle throughout our lives are fears with which we weren't born. These personal fears developed and were embedded at various points in our lives based on our own experiences or on the experiences of others with whom we were familiar.

To me, that's good news. It means if we develop most fear ourselves, then we can control—perhaps even eliminate completely—this fear through self-effort. Those who have developed a fear of flying, snakes, speaking in public, or whatever can consciously isolate and address those fears, working eventually to overcome and eliminate them.

Of course, the better option would be to never allow unnecessary fears (and let's face it, most of our fears are truly unnecessary) to develop in the first place. Over the years,

I've watched as potentially great leaders allowed unreasonable, unnecessary fears to stunt, stall, or scuttle their own professional growth and advancement. Three such universal fears are rejection, failure, and—as implausible as it sounds—even the fear of success.

The Fear of Rejection

Too many weak-willed leaders tend to recoil upon hearing the faintest catcalls of criticism regarding their decisions or intentions. Even one or two people on the fringe proclaiming meekly, "If I was in charge, you'd never catch me doing it that way" can be enough to create unfounded fears of widespread rejection in their minds. If they embrace this fear of rejection—of being isolated or marginalized—they may ultimately avoid, delay, or abandon altogether some very worthy initiatives or undertakings. These leaders are simply unwilling to move forward in the face of even minimal criticism or possible rejection.

Remember that critics are rarely, if ever, leaders themselves. The most vocal detractors can seldom lay claim to having accomplished anything resembling a progressive act that was not specifically assigned or required of them. Yet, they are sometimes the quickest to criticize the actions of those who are willing to step up and take action. They are, as Ernest Hemingway once declared, "people who watch a battle from a high place, then come down and shoot the survivors." That's not the way I'd like to be remembered as a leader—and I certainly don't wish such individuals to negatively influence me in that way.

It's never wise to fear rejection by the handful of people who might criticize your leadership actions. If you absolutely must fear something, I suggest you fear rejection less and instead fear the kind of professional insignificance that's brought on by hesitancy, complacency, and inactivity.

The Fear of Failure

Over the years, I've encountered a number of otherwise capable leaders who simply refused to try anything that was new and unproven—regardless how badly they or their organization needed a new approach or technique. Their fear of failing was so deep-seated that they consciously chose to do nothing significant. Their mind-set was essentially: "If I don't try or undertake anything that hasn't already been proved to be successful, then I can't possibly fail at it."

Of course, the sad truth is just the opposite. If leaders are willing to do only that which has been proved, assured, or commonplace, then they've already failed in their practical role as a leader. Don't get me wrong; I'm not suggesting that leaders should be riverboat gamblers, prone to betting the family farm on the luck of the dice. However, I do believe the most effective leaders are calculated risk takers who are practiced in the art of decision analysis. These folks don't purposely seek failure, but they do know that with risk comes reward. They therefore realize that occasional setbacks and continuing course corrections are predictable parts of blazing any new trail. Thus, such leaders move forward purposefully, prepared for—not paralyzed by—the possibility of occasionally failing along the way.

The Fear of Success

The most improbable fear of all may be fear of success. Years ago, I was talking with a young female professional about a job opportunity within her organization. The position would've provided her a significant increase in salary, responsibility, visibility, and unlimited future opportunities. I remember our conversation well.

"Sarah, you are interested in that position, aren't you?" I asked.

"No, I don't think so," she said, ever so casually.

"Really?" I responded, genuinely surprised. "You're the perfect candidate with the perfect skill set. You have the education, experience, technical skills, people skills—you've got all the tools necessary to be successful in that position."

"Yeah, I know."

"You know? Then why don't you pursue it?" I asked incredulously.

"Phil, I'm completely confident that I could be very successful in the job. However, as soon as I got good at it, they'd probably want to move me up to the next level—and I'm not sure what they'd expect of me then. I think I'll just stay where I am."

Read her words again. Nowhere does she overtly mention the fear of failing. In fact, she was supremely confident in her ability to perform at the next level. However, uncertainty about the unknown—and her own fear of what future success might look like—was the only barrier between her and (almost certain) future successes.

Leaders need to be especially mindful of these personal fears and their debilitating effects. The unwillingness to take appropriate risk—or the fear of speaking up in public, making a decision and acting on it, challenging tradition (the norm) in favor of improvement, the fear of necessary confrontation, not to mention countless others—can contribute to our fear of future successes. Along with many other fundamental leadership responsibilities and expectations, leaders need to embrace this awareness—not dread, avoid, or fear it.

"What Means 'Nervous'?"

My family and I were attending our weekly worship service one Sunday morning many years ago when we heard an interesting announcement. Our church would be starting an in-house musical academy that offered instruction in piano, guitar, violin, and vocal performance. Sophie, our four-year-old, immediately informed us that she wanted to join. My wife and I were leery of the idea. We knew she loved to sing, but was she old enough? Was she mature enough? Was she talented enough? Would it be a waste of time and money?

After several weeks of receiving our young daughter's near-constant encouragement, we gave in and contacted the music academy staff regarding their policy on accepting four-year-olds. Though predictably hesitant, the instructor agreed to give it a try. Sophie soon began taking weekly classes. After a few months, she proudly announced that her spring recital had been scheduled.

Almost immediately, I began to get nervous for her. I knew that singing behind closed doors to an instructor was one thing. Singing in front of an audience of strangers was something else entirely. However, I kept my concerns to myself.

The day of the recital finally arrived. The room was crowded with friends and family members of the budding musicians. Boys and girls, young men and women, some three, four, even five times Sophie's age, played, strummed, and sang with varying degrees of proficiency for those in attendance.

When the time came for our now four-and-a-half-year-old to take the stage, she marched confidently forward, took her spot, and nodded the signal for the pianist to begin. Three minutes later, she finished both verses of "On the Good Ship Lollipop" to enthusiastic audience response. Sophie acknowledged the applause with a practiced bow and demure smile before returning to her seat. I was one proud Papa.

That night as my wife tucked Sophie into bed, she took the opportunity to brag on our daughter and her performance once more.

"Sophie, you did so good today," she said encouragingly.

"Thanks, Mom. But you know what? I was a little nervous," she admitted.

"Well, Sophie, it's natural to be a little nervous when you're doing something new. But we couldn't tell. You did great. Anyway, you go to sleep. You've had a big day."

Susan was headed out of the room until Sophie called her back.

"Momma, I have a question. What means 'nervous'?" she asked innocently.

I believe my daughter experienced what many leaders also encounter in their jobs and responsibilities. After having so many people ask her if she was nervous in the days leading up to the recital, she felt almost obligated to be so—despite the fact that she had no real idea of what the concept meant or why she should embrace it. In other words, well-meaning individuals had begun to unintentionally transfer their personal fears related to public performance into the mind and psyche of an impressionable child.

Imagine the difference these same supporters could've made if they'd asked, "Sophie, are you excited?" rather than "Sophie, are you nervous?" Had they emphasized the positive aspects of her upcoming public performance, she would've likely stayed focused on those positives.

Leaders must be wary of the same psychological trap. There are many people who'll never be able to lead anything or anyone. They don't have the desire, intellect, or constitution for it. That doesn't make them bad people; it just means they'll never be leaders. You must accept that for what it is—and then refuse to allow them to plant unreasonable fears in your mind by transferring their personal inadequacies and biases regarding leadership to you.

If you possess a passion to make a difference in and through the lives of others, if you've trained and prepared yourself to perform the task at hand, if you're willing to stand up and step forward when called upon, then fear and nervousness should mean nothing to you.

Fearsome Fact #2: Unfamiliar Experiences Are Breeding Grounds for New Fears

Because it's a safe bet that almost everyone has had an unpleasant encounter with a mosquito at one time or another, let's talk about mosquitoes.

Have you ever wondered why mosquitoes live near you, causing you aggravation and ruining your outdoor activities? It's really very simple. Mosquitoes reside near you—possibly right in your yard—not because they have a personal vendetta against you, but rather because they've discovered favorable breeding grounds.

Most people know that mosquitoes need standing water to breed. What most people don't know is that lakes, ponds, and swamps, though attractive, are not absolutely necessary to accommodate the amorous, reproductive activities of those little buggers (pardon the pun). Obscure no-tell motels (nesting areas) for mosquitoes can also include neglected swimming pools, clogged roof gutters, abandoned tires, and even old tin cans—anywhere a little water can pool and stand. Entomologists advise that the only practical way to rid ourselves of the mosquito is via breeding site reduction.

It may seem unusual at best and ridiculous at worst to use the pesky mosquito as some sort of illustrative tool in the discussion of what *Leaders Ought to Know*. But think about it. Mosquitoes are a source of aggravation—and they're here to stay. But why should we promote their advancement by allowing unnecessary breeding sites to flourish?

Fears are also an aggravation, and they, too, are here to stay. But we should not promote ready breeding grounds for new fears to grow and flourish.

The truth is that most leaders anticipate the big breeding grounds and fears that can grow out of corporate ownership changes, internal management reorganizations, or pension plan restructuring. But the very best leaders anticipate and take care of the little things by exercising small breeding site reduction. They do so through activities like responding to follower inquiries promptly, inviting and valuing follower input, actively listening to follower concerns, and explaining internal process changes in a timely manner.

These leaders have learned that if you take care of the seemingly little things, the big things have a way of taking care of themselves. But if you don't work to take care of those little things while they're still little, they tend to ultimately grow and breed into bigger fears and challenges and then occupy an inordinate amount of our time and energy.

Making Unknowns Known

One of the most important things you can do as a leader is to recognize those things that can frighten you and your followers. For example, I frequently hear comments and discussions concerning fear of change, and I'm sorry but I just don't buy it. Change is one of the most common and anticipated aspects of human life. Life itself is a never-ending progression of changes. As a result, change is something with which every person becomes inherently and intimately familiar. We may not all like change, but we certainly learn to adapt to it and live with it.

No, it's not change that people fear; rather, the frightening aspects are the unknowns associated with those changes. Your followers don't fear getting you as their new boss. Chances are they've had several bosses before you and they've adapted to each one. But they might initially fear the unknowns that come with you as their new boss. They want to know your leadership style, your work habits, your communication skills, what you expect of them, and so on. As they come to know these unknowns, people will predictably relinquish their fears and adapt to life's changes.

As a leader, one of your primary responsibilities is to work diligently to make your followers' unknowns known—thus releasing them from the burden of their personal fear. Conversely, as someone who may occasionally fear the unknowns in your own life and work, you must work diligently to find the currently unknown answers to your questions.

By the way, fear of the unknown is a wonderfully fertile plot in which the weed of worry can take root and grow. I personally define *worry* as unproductive use of one's imagination. In other words, we tend to use our imaginations to create what-if scenarios that have very little, if any, connection to reality. Therefore, if worry is unproductive use of one's imagination, then it seems reasonable to assert that planning must be the opposite: a productive use of one's imagination.

Another way to think about it is this: If something is worth worrying about, then it's worth planning for. However, if it's not worth planning for, why are you worrying about it?

Yes, I realize I said earlier that unfamiliar experiences are the breeding grounds for new fears. But no, I'm not suggesting we forgo or avoid any unfamiliar experiences simply for the purpose of eliminating potential new fears for our followers or ourselves. That's not practical. The world is changing every day in various ways. If we're not open to such changes, we will be easily swept away by the waves of insignificance and irrelevance.

What I am suggesting is that every leader be purposefully aware of his or her responsibility to make their followers' unknowns known—and to do so in as timely, methodical, and unemotional a way as possible.

Simply put, *Leaders Ought to Know* that whatever time they invest up front in making followers' unknowns known will yield huge dividends by avoiding or eliminating the residual effect associated with frightened followers.

Fearsome Fact #3: Unsuccessful Experiences Compound Our Fears

A few pages ago, I related the story of my four-year-old daughter, her passion for singing and her total disregard for fear as it manifested itself in nervousness.

Sophie continued to use and develop her considerable vocal talents past that first recital, never shying away from public performances. She sang at school events, during church services, at local talent shows, and as a member of an all-state choir that toured for six straight summers. Sophie loved singing—and she was good at it.

About age 11, Sophie was asked to sing a solo during our church's annual children's choir performance. By this time, Sophie had performed on dozens of occasions in a variety of environments. But this opportunity was to be special for her. She was to be featured in her home church, performing with choir members made up of friends and classmates.

She practiced her solo constantly for weeks, singing her part so frequently that I eventually felt qualified to be her understudy. She was prepared. She wanted to do well. And I was confident she would.

As with most amateur productions, the evening of the performance was chaotic. Sophie and two other soloists arrived early to be fitted with individual microphones; however, the sound tests were canceled due to the overflow of early arriving concert-goers.

The performance began with the entire choir in full voice, supported by a full array of instrumental accompaniment. As Sophie's solo approached, the choir reached its full crescendo before falling completely silent in anticipation of Sophie's vocal offering.

Then, disaster struck.

Sophie confidently hit her first note to begin her solo—but with absolutely no voice amplification. As it turned out, her microphone was dead. Though she struggled mightily to project, her young voice was no match for the cavernous auditorium. Barely a soul in the audience could hear and appreciate her effort.

The heads of young choir members jerked to look in her direction. Nervous giggles broke out. Adult audience members lurched forward in their seats, straining to hear and then mumbling rudely to their neighbors when they couldn't. A general buzz overtook the venue, drowning out Sophie's voice completely. Meanwhile, the volunteers in the sound booth frantically switched levers and whirled knobs in an effort to restore power and sound to Sophie's microphone.

Eventually, Sophie's microphone squealed back to life, capturing and magnifying the last few notes of her solo, just before the choir was to resume. No additional sound problems were experienced. But for Sophie, the damage was done. As her father, I suffered along with her. Her body language told the story. She was crushed.

When the concert ended, I went forward to reassure her. As Sophie and many others, young and old, milled about on stage, I walked up just in time to hear one of Sophie's classmates loudly proclaim to all that would listen, "The concert would've been great if Sophie hadn't messed up her part."

Sophie's devastation was complete and profound. Though the microphone malfunction was obviously not her fault, she chose to take the personal criticism to heart. It's fairly easy to imagine the hurt that one thoughtless comment can cause. We've all felt the immediate sting that can be inflicted by someone's sharp tongue. Words do matter. But sometimes we fail to consider the long-lasting, residual damage that can be done by a single unsuccessful experience and the unnecessary attention that is called to it.

As a result, that was Sophie's last public solo for seven years. The little girl who loved singing more than anything else in her life voluntarily chose to have her voice silenced due to the unpleasant memory of one unsuccessful experience— and the negative attention that it elicited.

What It Means

Can you see the connection between an impressionable 11-year-old's unsuccessful experience in front of her audience and, let's say, a 30-year-old supervisor's unsuccessful experience of some sort in front of his? I hope so. The culprit that is negatively influencing both is the same—fear. And its long-term effects can be profoundly damaging, whatever the scenario—and whomever its victim.

As leaders, we must recognize and do battle with those fears that inhabit our minds and our workplaces. Remember, young or old, male or female, experienced or inexperienced— we all have fears. They slip into our camp disguised as unfamiliar or unsuccessful experiences, and if left to their own dubious devices, they can deconstruct, derail, and ultimately destroy the good that leaders and followers can otherwise do together.

Fear is a leader's enemy. *Leaders Ought to Know* that we can defeat and overcome fear; however, the battle lines must be drawn now. You must commit to facing and resisting your fears whenever and wherever you encounter them. Most important of all, you must never retreat from your fears. To do so is to admit defeat.

Yes, fear is a leader's enemy, but it can be quickly joined by other leadership pitfalls that we must also recognize, acknowledge, and eradicate. The following chapter takes up that challenge.

Chapter 10

Leadership Pitfalls

Ground Rule #10

Leaders' wounds shouldn't be self-inflicted;

Leaders flourish when serious errors of judgment are avoided.

Seven Deadly Sins

For much of recorded history, theologians, philosophers, sociologists, politicians, authors, and even thespians have observed, pondered, evaluated, and commented on the human condition—and they've often fixed their focus on our principal flaws. These intimate examinations of human life, behavior, and activity have revealed a common predisposition toward universal sins—serious errors in judgment—that predictably repeat themselves again and again, generation after generation.

In the 1995 film thriller *Seven,* starring Brad Pitt, Morgan Freeman, and a cast of other notable actors, a sadistic serial killer justifies his carefully planned murders as absolution for the world's ignorance of the human imperfections known as the seven deadly sins. These sins have been a central part of formal Christian religious education, instruction, and inspiration for millions of people worldwide for hundreds of years. As such, they are familiar to those who embrace faith-based concepts—as well as those who don't. In case your memory is a bit foggy, I'll remind you that the seven are:

- Wrath
- Greed
- Sloth
- Pride
- Lust
- Envy
- Gluttony

These have long been identified as personal transgressions that are fatal to spiritual progress. But some similar professional transgressions can prove equally fatal to leadership progress. These workplace transgressions include anger (wrath), selfishness (greed), laziness (sloth), arrogance (pride), covetousness (lust), jealousy (envy), and excessiveness of all sorts (gluttony).

Though significant sins—serious errors in leadership judgment—unquestionably exist, I'm unwilling to restrict the number to 7, 17, or even 70 times 7. Frankly, there are more ways to ruin leadership influence and effectiveness than I can name or explore here.

So as we strive to bind people together—rather than drive them apart—it's important to recognize, avoid, and, whenever necessary, correct attitudes and behaviors that are universally undesirable, even contemptible, in our followers' eyes. Whether we call them sins, transgressions, or simply pitfalls (which is my preference here), three primary ones exist.

Leadership Pitfall #1: An Elevated Sense of Self-Importance

There've been a number of times over the years when one of my program participants felt inclined to tell me what a good job he or she was doing as a leader. These conversations tend to be one-on-one and out of others' sight and earshot. Each time I find myself in such a conversation, I try to be respectful and listen attentively. However, I must admit that I always catch myself thinking the same thought:

Don't you realize that it doesn't really matter that you *think of yourself as a good leader? What's far more important is what* your followers *think about you as their leader.* That's *what you should be most concerned about.*

Power and position can be an awesome combination. It has the potential to accomplish much good for the organization, followers, and even the leader. Unfortunately, an elevated sense of self-importance (aka pride, arrogance, conceit, haughtiness, overconfidence, condescension) can surreptitiously destroy whatever positive leadership goodwill you may possess or have stockpiled over time.

One of two things usually happens when individuals are elevated into positions of leadership and responsibility: Newly designated leaders either grow or they swell. Growth is good. It's positive and desirable. Swelling, on the other hand, can be considered the first step toward any living organism rotting and ruining. Need I go further with this analogy? I think you get the picture.

As Scottish philosopher David Hume once said, "When men are the most sure and arrogant, they are commonly the most mistaken." Thinking yourself too important foretells any number of future problems—unwillingness to listen to others, inability to rally support around an idea or undertaking, powerlessness to influence or impact others' voluntary actions, incapability of making a lasting difference, and so on. Remember from Chapter 3: The essential element of leadership has been, is, and always will be your followers. If we constantly work to make our followers feel most important, they'll be more apt to assure that we are.

"I Hope the Old Man Is Getting Some of This"

Eighty-five top managers from a well-known national organization were jammed into a hotel meeting room for a one-day leadership retreat. I'd been invited to kick off the day by guiding the group in a three-hour discussion about leadership.

The room was completely full, configured classroom style, with the chairs and tables equally distributed. The attendees were divided by a wide aisle running from the front of the room to the exit doors in the back. I worked from the front on a raised platform.

I wanted to get the group involved as quickly as possible, so I began with a simple exercise. First, I asked them to think of the best leader they'd ever known. I then asked each to write down the characteristics that specific leader possessed that made him or her a memorable leader. Finally, one-by-one, I had participants read their lists out loud to give everyone an idea of the leadership characteristics they'd all witnessed and found valuable over time. I had used this exercise many times over the years (described in detail in Chapter 4, "A Recipe for Respect") and with many different audiences—each time with great success. I had no reason to believe this instance would be any different.

As one participant after another publicly shared their notes, I scrawled each individual offering on a flip chart for all to see. There was an upbeat energy in the room as this compilation of positive attributes expanded before our eyes. It was obvious that those present were enjoying and actively engaged in the exercise.

I'd logged more than two dozen leadership characteristics on the flip chart in less than 30 minutes, and people still had more they were waiting to share. But then, something unexpected happened. In an instant, the activity went from one of great promise to one of great concern.

As I faced the audience, in the front-row seat closest to the aisle on my left sat the group's chief executive officer. Up to that point, he'd been participating actively in the exercise. Suddenly, with no prior warning, the CEO laid his pen down and pushed himself away from the table. He then leaned back in his chair and spoke in a voice loud enough to be heard throughout the room. "Yeah," he said, through a self-satisfied sigh, "I think it's obvious I do all those things."

Immediately, at least 75 percent of the eyes in that room dropped, searching for that invisible spot on the table in front of them. It was as if people didn't dare look directly at one another.

As their eyes dropped, their mouths shut—and then that was it. No one had anything else to say—*nothing!* Just moments before, there had been active group participation; suddenly, there was abject silence.

Admittedly concerned that such a mood would hang over the final hour and a half of the session, I knew I had to act quickly and regroup to avert further damage. There was simply no way I could tap-dance through another 90 minutes of dismal group silence. I announced a 10-minute break in the action. Relieved to be able to escape the suddenly uncomfortable environment, the group as a whole was instantly out of their chairs and moving into the aisle, heading toward the back doors.

That is, all but one young man. He stood firmly planted in the middle of the aisle, not moving at all. His colleagues flowed around him like rushing water around a boulder in a stream. All the while he stood still, transfixed, staring downward, lost deep in thought.

I was immediately intrigued. This guy's observable behavior stood in stark contrast to that of his colleagues. *What's on his mind?* I wondered. I wanted to know more.

Cautiously, respectfully, I moved closer to where the young man stood, careful not to invade his personal space or thoughts. My plan was to be immediately available, should he wish to share his thoughts with me. I sauntered alongside, stopped and waited. Apparently, it was enough.

The young man finally looked up and took a couple of steps toward me. He never came to a complete stop, choosing instead to glide by my side inconspicuously. But in passing, he leaned in and shared what I was convinced was the primary thought occupying his mind.

"I hope the old man is getting some of this," he said, with a note of disgust in his voice.

Of course, by "the old man," I was convinced he was referring to the CEO. And his stated hope led me to believe that—despite the CEO's elevated opinion of himself and his self-perceived leadership strengths and abilities—not all his would-be followers concurred with that opinion.

With his emotional burden lightened a bit, the young man moved on, joining his colleagues for the break.

Elevated self-importance is an unnecessary wound and one that's too often self-inflicted. For those leaders truly committed to making a lasting difference, the words of legendary football coach Vince Lombardi ring true: "Individual commitment to a group effort—that is what makes a team work, a company work, a society work, a civilization work."

The best leaders know that it's not "me"; it's "we."

Leadership Pitfall #2: Practicing Favoritism

Let me ask you a tough question. Do you have a favorite employee or team member? There's no benefit in kidding yourself now, so be honest. Do you have a favorite employee?

Forgive me for being so presumptuous, but I already know the answer. Of course, you have a favorite—maybe even more than one. We all do! Our natural likes and dislikes mean that each of us is drawn to one person over another, whatever the relationship—between a teacher and a student, a member of the clergy and a parishioner, a coach and a team member, and, yes, even a leader and a follower.

I'm not referring to some sort of illicit, immoral, illegal, or even unethical relationship. This is just Human Nature 101; simply put, it's natural to like some people better than others, for any number of different reasons. But it's tough to admit that fact publicly (even privately), isn't it? Just thinking about admitting it causes us to cringe at the possibility of the negative backlash from those who are the not-so favorites, should they ever learn our true feelings.

But that's the point. They already know.

In an effort to examine the favoritism issue a bit more carefully, we should ask ourselves what it is that makes one person a favorite over another. Is it formal education or a specific level of specialized training? Is it age, maturity, or years of service? Could it be physical looks or attractiveness? No, none of these ring true—at least not for the professional leader.

I firmly believe the universal determinant of who becomes the leader's workplace favorite is essentially a question of who consistently gets their job done with the least amount of direct supervision, organizational drama, and overall disruption. I'm betting you agree. It's very likely that the person who's able to get the work done while making your life easier in the process will be—or already is—your hands-down favorite, too.

So being your favorite is a good thing for that chosen golden child, right? As a reward for diligence and hard work, your favorite can expect to be rewarded with the cushiest jobs and most favorable assignments, right? The uninformed might expect so, but the reality is often radically different.

Too often, the rewards awaiting the favorite include heavier workloads, longer hours, more difficult assignments, and loftier expectations. I like to think of such a scenario as reverse favoritism—that situation in which the favored employees get the least favored treatment.

Conversely, leaders often release those employees who moan, groan, gripe, and complain the loudest—about even the most minimal or insignificant tasks, assignments, or requests—from their professional expectations and obligations far too often. Why? Honestly, more often than not, the leader just gets tired of listening to it all. Once the gripers realize that their griping allows them to do less, not more, they're sure to continue and intensify this behavior. Remember, that which gets rewarded gets repeated.

I suggested back in Chapter 7, "Why People Do What They Do," that the second piece of the motivational puzzle was that "people will generally focus on and take the easiest route available to satisfy their needs."

Considering all the griping that leaders hear, many assume—and rightly so—that it's simply easier to ask their favorites to do the job. Easier because, over time, we've come to expect our favorites to do what we ask without question, reservation, conflict, or confrontation. And that is usually what happens, until our favorites eventually get a belly full of their favored treatment.

Leaders Ought to Know the practical difference between having favorites and showing favoritism. Common sense reminds us of how crucial it is to set performance standards high and then make sure that everyone, not just your favorites, performs at the expected level. Otherwise, you may begin to see those favorites either slipping away from you in search of greener pastures or, worse still, gradually joining the ranks of the gripers and complainers that surround us.

"I'd Rather Be Flat Broke"

It was the first time I ever remember Claude coming into my office. I was surprised to see him standing in my doorway.

About age 50, he'd worked at the plant as a skilled machine operator for almost nine years. I'd been the human resources manager at that manufacturing operation for two of those nine years. During that period, Claude and I had established a good working relationship. By nature, he was very quiet, not talkative at all, preferring instead to keep to himself and do his job in relative seclusion. Though he preferred the low-key approach, Claude took great pride in his job and his advanced level of workmanship.

"Excuse me, Phil. I'd like to speak to you for a moment, if that's possible," he said politely, his voice low and slow.

"Sure, Claude. C'mon in and sit down. What's on your mind?" I asked.

"I'd really like to know what the plans are for getting me some backup support on my machine. As you probably know, I've been working a whole lot of overtime recently. Now, please don't get me wrong; I'm thankful to have this job. It's just that I'm getting pretty beat down by the excessive hours. I know it'll take a while to train somebody to do this job, and I'm certainly willing to do that. I'd just like to be able to tell my family that they'll be able to see a little more of me sometime soon."

Claude was describing a unique situation. He was a highly skilled senior machine operator. In fact, he was the best we had. Because of his advanced skill, he'd been our only operator working on a highly sophisticated, low-volume, high-profit product for the last couple of years. But orders for that product had spiked in recent months—and since Claude was the only operator trained to produce the product to fill those orders, overtime was unavoidable. I was aware of the increased production schedule but unaware of just how much overtime Claude had been assigned.

"How much overtime are you talking about?" I asked.

"Well, this week will mark more than 20 straight days of at least 12-hour shifts," he replied calmly. I was surprised.

"I had no idea you'd been working that many hours," I admitted. "How about if I talk to Don and then get back to you after that with an answer?"

"That's fine," he said, before heading out the door to return to work.

Later that day, I found our production manager, Don, and told him about my meeting with Claude. He was well aware of the current dilemma, for Claude and the company, and he confessed that he didn't know what to do about it. Because he couldn't predict how long the specialty orders would remain at their current level, Don was hesitant to hire or train a second machine operator for fear the current order volume wouldn't sustain itself. He didn't know what to do next. Don thanked me for bringing the issue to his attention and assured me he would take it from there and discuss the matter further with Claude, seeking some sort of short-term resolution. I didn't think any more about it.

About two weeks later, I looked up to see Claude standing in my doorway once again.

"Hey, Claude, c'mon in and sit down," I said casually.

"No thanks," he replied in a matter-of-fact tone. "I won't be here that long. I'm just here to give you my two weeks' notice. Two weeks from today will be my last day."

I was shocked. "Quitting? Why? Have you accepted another job?" I asked.

"No, I don't have another job to go to. I'm quitting because you didn't do what you told me you'd do," he responded. "And I don't want to work for a company that takes their employees for granted, especially the ones who try to do a good job."

I felt blindsided by the accusation. I tried to explain that I had, in fact, spoken with Don concerning Claude's situation as I'd promised I would. However, he was right. I hadn't gotten back to him as I said I would—and, apparently, neither had Don. I was embarrassed. I'd dropped the ball. But I didn't want my foolish mistake to cost Claude or the company. I was desperate not to lose one of our very best employees unnecessarily. Though it was really none of my business, I asked Claude a rather personal question.

"Claude, can you really afford to just walk away from this job without another one to go to?"

His reply was simple, to the point and quite emphatic. "Phil, the best I can figure, I've got about two months of savings set aside to last me until I can find my next job," he said, before adding, "but I'd rather be flat broke than work for a company that cares so little about its employees."

Claude was a man of his word. Two weeks later, he turned in his keys and safety gear and walked away. As you've probably guessed, he continued to work the overtime assigned him during his last 14 days of employment with us—with his same commitment to quality production and without additional complaint. He was a consummate professional right up to the time of his departure.

As for Don and me, one fact was inescapable: We'd taken unfair advantage (albeit unintentionally) of one of our best and most dedicated employees, and it ended up costing us dearly. Claude moved on to his next professional challenge, where I was sure he would continue his conscientious ways. We, on the other hand, immediately began the process of hiring two inexperienced operators to take the place of one master operator. Ironically, we ended up doing the very thing that Claude—our favorite—had asked of us in the first place. Unfortunately, we were several weeks late in doing so. And neither of the men now sharing this load was of the caliber of the expert we'd regrettably lost.

Claude's story should serve as a cautionary tale for all leaders. Why? Because many leaders—just like you and me—can easily find ourselves in a similar situation. Reverse favoritism is a pitfall that you can and should identify—and correct.

Leadership Pitfall #3: Inability or Unwillingness to Control Emotions

Emotion is an undeniable aspect of both the human and leadership experience. However, my claim that a key leadership pitfall is the inability or unwillingness to control emotions should never be interpreted as a suggestion that all emotions are bad. They're not. Emotions are a wonderful part of life and leadership. If either lacked emotion, we'd be in for an extremely boring and monotonous existence.

Never should a leader be devoid of emotion. The last thing any organization needs is a zombie, a robot, a Mr. Spock knockoff masquerading as a leader of men and women. Emotion is good; we should embrace it. But we must also manage it appropriately. With that singular thought in mind, I offer this critical piece of advice:

Share your emotions; don't show them.

For those who are wondering what the difference might be, it's a pretty simple concept, really. It's just not the first thing that most leaders think to do. When you feel yourself getting angry, instead of showing your anger in ways that might lead to a loss of control, share your anger. Tell the people with whom you're involved that you're angry and why.

Instead of showing your frustration, share your frustration with those who need to know. Explain the source and magnitude of your frustration with those who are either the cause of or affected by your frustration.

If you're experiencing fear for some reason, don't show your fear reaction, whatever that might be; instead, share your fears openly with those involved to make appropriate plans to combat and overcome those fears.

Remember, having the courage to talk openly and frankly about the emotions you're sure to experience is not a leadership weakness; it's a leadership strength. And it's one that some of us discover the hard way.

When You Lose Your Temper

I was entering a critical period in my professional development. I was about 23 years old, fresh out of college, a crisp new diploma in hand. I wanted to be a leader, but I had so much to learn.

My first supervisory position was as personnel supervisor in a facility that employed more than 300 workers. I reported to the director of human resources and was at least partially responsible for employee-related decisions involving hiring, firing, promotion, demotion, training, and discipline.

The job was an important one. I had a significant amount of institutional power. I knew it, as did others in the organization—and, honestly, I liked it. In fact, I began to like it too much. Though it's uncomfortable to admit it now, I developed a big head—an elevated sense of self-worth and importance (see "Leadership Pitfall #1: An Elevated Sense of Self-Importance"). I began to think more highly of myself than my knowledge, skills, or experience warranted. Little did I know that a huge leadership lesson was looming on the horizon.

I was working in my office when an employee, John, walked in unannounced, sat down, and, without invitation, began sharing a problem. It was obvious from the outset that John had no intention of working to solve this particular problem. His undisguised purpose was to pass his problem off to me.

The underlying but unspoken truth of the moment was that I didn't care about John's problem—and, frankly, I didn't like John. Becoming ever more aggravated by his

221

Leadership Pitfalls

presumptuous attitude (and ignoring my own)—combined with my own overestimated sense of power and control—the storm clouds of confrontation began to gather in my mind.

The more I listened, the angrier I got. I sat and began to fantasize about what I would like to say to John, even as John continued to speak. Ignorant as I was of the consequences to follow, I soon stopped fantasizing and started planning what I would say if he kept talking. Unfortunately, my thoughts ultimately morphed into action as I began to tell John exactly what I thought of him and his trivial little problem. I unloaded, holding nothing back.

But what John did next surprised me. *He told me what he thought of me!* I wasn't expecting that, and I was highly indignant.

How dare he talk to me that way! I thought. *Doesn't he recognize who I am? Doesn't he recognize I could get him fired?*

Apparently, my position—and the presumed power it held—didn't faze John one bit. He lashed out quickly and vigorously. In fact, I now know that I should've predicted his response to my aggressive attack. When someone launches an attack on another, you must expect a defensive counterattack. It's natural. It's going to happen, in one way or another.

Nevertheless, in that moment, I found myself embroiled in an unanticipated verbal free-for-all. It didn't last long, less than five minutes total. However, I still contend the damage we inflicted with our tongues during that brief encounter produced deeper scars than could've been produced with our fists in that same period of time.

Then it was over, ending as quickly as it began. With our personal attacks complete and our emotional loads sufficiently dumped, John stormed out of my office, slamming the door behind him.

In truth, the experience was far from over. As long as the memory of an unpleasant experience lives on, the experience itself is alive in the consciousness of those involved and affected.

As you surely know, news travels fast inside organizations—and bad news travels even faster. There was no question that my boss would hear about this encounter. The only real question was when.

I got the answer to that question within 15 minutes with the ringing of my office phone.

"Hello," I growled, still fueled by the volatile cocktail of anger, pride, and adrenaline.

The voice on the line was calm and measured. It belonged to my boss, Jerry. "Phil, come on over to my office. There are a couple of things we need to talk about."

I knew what Jerry wanted, of course. I also knew I wasn't in any mood to take a tongue lashing or butt chewing. Still emotionally ramped up—not to mention immature and arrogant—I readied myself for a second fight.

I'm not gonna take any of his crap, I thought. *There are plenty of organizations that would appreciate my considerable talents. I was looking for a job when I found this one.*

Already possessing an arrogant attitude, I gathered a full head of steam as I walked from my office to Jerry's. As I made my approach, another thought flashed through my mind.

This is his meeting. He called it. If he wants to talk, he can talk. I'm not saying a word.

I entered Jerry's office, and he directed me to take a seat. I sat down across the desk from him, assuming a seated posture that would have indicated to even the least informed individual that I was feeling far from remorseful.

Jerry paused and looked me in the eye before speaking. His facial expression and body language were relaxed, neutral, without obvious aggression.

"Phil, I understand you had a little bit of a problem awhile ago" were his exact words. They were delivered without a hint of emotion, absent both sarcasm and accusation.

Despite Jerry's calm demeanor, my emotions were still far too close to the surface. They showed up quickly in my instinctive response to his opening statement.

"Yeah," I barked angrily.

But Jerry didn't strike at the emotional bait. He could've. He could've said, "Wait a minute, son. Who do you think you're talking to? I'm your boss, remember? I'm not going to be disrespected that way. Your tone is bordering on insubordination. You better straighten up right now."

No, he didn't say those words or any like them. Jerry knew me, his follower—and he knew full well that I was not being intentionally disrespectful in that moment, but that I was emotionally vulnerable. He knew the wrong word could lead our meeting in the wrong direction. Most important, he knew what needed to be done and he had a plan to make it happen. And he stuck to his plan.

Jerry picked up a pad of notebook paper from his desk, leaned back in his chair, and started writing, in silence, on the pad. I, too, sat silently, not terribly interested in what he was writing—or anything else at that moment. Soon enough, Jerry

Leaders Ought to Know

leaned forward in his chair and, still without speaking a word, slid the entire pad of paper across the desk to me.

It was obvious he wanted me to read what he'd written. I picked up the pad and read five words—the only five words on the page:

WHEN YOU LOSE YOUR TEMPER

I read the words but didn't understand their meaning. I reread the stark message a couple of more times before finally, silently, sliding the pad back across the desk.

Jerry retrieved the pad and began writing again. It didn't take long this time. When finished, he slid the pad back across the desk. I retrieved the pad and immediately noticed that three of the original words had been marked out. Two words remained:

~~WHEN~~ YOU LOSE ~~YOUR TEMPER~~

I looked at Jerry. He began to speak. "You lose, boy," he said evenly but with conviction. "But what's most important right now is not that you lost, but rather that you understand exactly what it is that you've lost. Just a little while ago, you lost your credibility, integrity, and professionalism—all in less than five minutes."

Jerry continued. "Phil, you have no idea how many times over the past year or so people have told me that you were too young for your position. I've told them repeatedly not to judge you on your age, but rather on your accomplishments. And until today, you've made me proud."

Jerry paused, watching me carefully and allowing ample time for his words to find their mark. Eventually, he followed with a question: "Phil, do you have any idea what John might be doing right now?"

"No, I don't," I answered. Those were the last words I would speak in the entire meeting.

As for the question itself, the truth was that I hadn't thought any more about John since the incident. The only person I'd been thinking about had been me!

"Well, let me tell you what John's doing. Right now he may be at his work station, or in the break room, or out in the parking lot—but wherever he is, you can be sure he's surrounded by people who're saying, 'I heard you got under Phil's skin today. Nobody else has done that. How'd you do it? I'd like to give it a try.' Oh yeah, Phil—you can be sure more people will try to get you riled up in the future. Why? Because after what happened today, they know you're vulnerable.

"Phil, you can be sure that I'll be hearing from some folks who'll want me to fire you. But I'm not going to do that this time. Frankly, I'm not going to discipline you in any way. After all, what could I do to you that would be worse than what you've already done to yourself and your reputation here? But you should also know that I'm not going to help you learn to control your temper. The only person who can do anything about that is you. My purpose for talking to you now is just to let you know exactly what it is that you've lost."

End of meeting.

It would be safe to assume that I left that meeting with a very different attitude than when I entered. I returned to my office and did some serious soul searching. Before the afternoon was over, I'd made a promise to myself that I've kept to this day—and that I intend to keep for the rest of my life.

I will never lose my temper in public again.

Have I been tempted to fly off the handle since that day? Absolutely! Do I still encounter situations that make me angry? Frequently! But now, when I feel the anger rising, when I feel my face and ears flush with emotion, when I feel the beads of perspiration form on my forehead and trickle down my spine—that's when I remember one of the most valuable leadership lessons I've ever learned. That's when I remember Jerry's words: *when you lose your temper—you lose!*

These seven words *always* elicit more immediate feedback from on-site program participants than any other single story I share, and for a long time, I wondered why that was. Was it because I tell it better than any other of my stories? Possibly, but I doubt it. Was it because people always like to see the tale teller get his comeuppance in the story? Maybe, but I have my doubts about that, too.

I've simply concluded over time that people respond the way they do to this story because, at one time or another, *all of us* have had the same experience I did. We've all screwed up royally by being unable to rein in our emotions: anger, frustration, fear, or whatever. It seems that the most valuable lessons for most of us—certainly, the ones we remember longest—are the ones that leave the most significant scars.

So, as we approach the end of this chapter, I have one more piece of advice for leaders. It's a crucial one to share as I attempt to steer you away from the ravages of leadership's pitfalls—especially those involving human emotion. If you find that you've fallen victim to one of these pitfalls, my advice is this: *Apologize—say you're sorry.*

The Power of an Apology

I couldn't possibly conclude this chapter without stressing the importance of apologizing. The fact is that we all have made mistakes and will continue to make mistakes on occasion. The mistakes aren't the important part. What we do immediately after making those mistakes is critical to how people will view not only the mistakes but also our leadership character, moving forward.

The act of apologizing is one of the most powerful tools available to leaders, yet it's also unfortunately one of the most seldom used. There seems to be a school of thought within a portion of the leadership community that suggests a personal apology is tantamount to admitting weakness, imperfection, ineffectiveness, inadequacy, impotence, or some other unseemly malady.

I respectfully disagree with this point of view.

I read an article several years ago that stated personal apologies are forthcoming only 47 percent of the time— *when they are deserved* (emphasis added). In other words, more than half the time, people deserving of an apology are left waiting—longing—for an apology that will never come.

I have no idea whether this 47 percent statistic is legitimate. Nevertheless, it got me thinking. What if leaders got into the habit of apologizing to their followers frequently—and sincerely— every time they made a mistake, large or small? Notice that I stress *sincerely;* I'm not talking about a half-hearted, while-the-camera-is-on-me, playing-to-the-grandstands kind of apology. I mean a genuine apology.

In *Crucial Conversations,* Chapter 5, "How to Make It Safe to Talk about Almost Anything," authors Kerry Patterson, Joseph Grenny, Ron McMillan, and Al Switzler write (p. 84): "An apology is a statement that sincerely expresses your sorrow for your role in causing—or at least not preventing pain or difficulty to others. . . . Now any apology isn't really an apology unless you experience a change of heart."

Some followers would probably be initially surprised to hear their leader apologize for something that caused them pain or difficulty. I'm guessing it would be a pleasant surprise that wouldn't take long to get used to. I'm also guessing—as a leader myself—that individual leaders would redouble their efforts over time to make sure they got things right so they wouldn't have to apologize to their followers so frequently. Either way, the quality goes up—and followers feel more appreciated.

Pursuing Leadership Success

A key step in solidifying your leadership position and reputation is to avoid the pitfalls that can entrap even the most experienced leaders. That's why this chapter is important; it's here to serve as a sort of cautionary tale.

However, to maximize the leadership potential that exists within you, you must pursue leadership success proactively and aggressively. The final chapter provides commonsense success strategies that *Leaders Ought to Know.*

Chapter 11

Commonsense Success

> **Ground Rule #11**
>
> Leaders don't always need to plow new ground;
>
> Leaders can watch, listen, and learn from the success of others.

Seniority, Experience, or Something Else?

Years ago, while still working as a corporate human resources manager, I was part of an executive team that faced a difficult managerial decision. We were responsible for deciding whether to promote a senior employee—an individual who possessed adequate knowledge and skills—or a promising junior employee who admittedly possessed less institutional knowledge and skills but had tremendous upside potential, as evidenced by her personal desire to learn, grow, and do.

After much deliberation, we opted for the latter. We simply believed the organization and its employees would be better served over time by the junior employee's leadership. As you might imagine, our decision did not sit well with the rejected employee.

"How can you make such a foolish decision?" he demanded to know.

The selection committee's chairperson pulled no punches in answering the employee's question. He spoke truthfully and to the point.

"You actually helped us make our decision by the attitude we've all seen you display over the years. You've consistently resisted most of the opportunities afforded you to learn, grow, and expand your influence and impact within this organization and industry. You've opted instead to put your own comfort and convenience ahead of the needs of those you might one day be charged with leading," the manager stated correctly. "Such an attitude is obvious to others and inconsistent with what we expect from our leaders going forward."

Faced with the truth yet frustrated by it, the desperate employee shot back, "So you just choose to ignore my almost 20 years of experience?"

The manager's response was again direct and on target.

"I won't argue that you have nearly 20 years with this organization. But you certainly don't have 20 years of experience. You only have a few years of experience—that period early on when you were still willing to learn and grow. However, you've consciously and voluntarily forfeited numerous opportunities to gain additional experience in more recent years. You've consistently chosen instead to be satisfied with where you are, what you know, and what you do."

Does any of this sound familiar? Do you know people who fall into this category?

I can write candidly about such people here with little fear of offending my readers because I know that people lacking personal desire stopped reading this book chapters ago—if indeed they ever started it. They possess no real desire to learn more about what *Leaders Ought to Know* because they've decided they know enough already. Their attitude indicates an inclination toward leadership complacency, not leadership excellence.

I've always believed personal desire to be the fuel that powers one's commitment and, ultimately, one's success. Show me an individual who has tremendous knowledge and skills but little or no personal desire to do or be more, and I'll show you a pitiful example of wasted potential. But show me an individual with limited knowledge and skills who still has an ample supply of desire, and I'll show you a success in the making.

Choosing Success

Over the years, I've developed a keen interest in what others have to say about the topic of personal and professional success. I've found that many folks define success based on what can be measured or quantified (e.g., money, position, or organizational influence), and others proclaim true success to be more a state of mind (e.g., happiness, satisfaction, or enlightenment).

Still other success seekers prefer more philosophical explanations, such as:

The magical philosophy: "Success is simply a matter of luck. Ask any failure."—Anonymous

The mystical philosophy: "When a man is willing and eager, the gods join in."—Anonymous

The fundamental philosophy: "Success is neither magical nor mysterious. Success is the natural consequence of consistently applying basic fundamentals."—Jim Rohn

Interesting? I think so. But none of these definitions adequately depicts my personal perspective on success. Rohn's assertion—that success is a consequence of consistently applied "basic fundamentals"—resonates most closely with me. I interpret it to mean that one can expect eventual success if one adheres to a commonsense approach.

But that, of course, begs the question—what is common sense? I've discovered those concepts, ideas, and techniques that have proven so valuable to me over the years—the things that now seem common sense—may not be all that *common* and may not make much *sense* to others. Therefore, we need to bridge that gap in understanding. To do so, I'll keep it simple and straightforward. I've discovered the path, pursuit, and realization of success is essentially an equation:

Success equals choices. Or stated in slightly broader terms: The more choices I have, the more successful I tend to be; the fewer choices I have, the more limited my success.

Too Many Choices?

It's amazing how many times I hear leaders publicly bemoan the number of choices they face, often saying things like:

"I wish someone would tell me where to start. . . ."

"So many things need my attention, it's hard to know what to do next. . . ."

"I would enjoy my life so much more if there weren't so many options to choose from. . . ."

From my perspective, people who make these kinds of statements have it all wrong. Instead of grumbling about the quantity and variety of the choices available, they should enthusiastically celebrate as they count, not gripe about, the choices before them.

I know you may be thinking, *Phil, I don't mean to be ungrateful. But you must admit, having so many choices to decide between can be so overwhelming that it becomes stressful!*

Of course, I recognize and acknowledge that fact. But I would argue that not having choices can be personally stressful as well. Which would you prefer? Having the right and opportunity to choose the direction you will go or having such choices withheld from or dictated to you? It's hard for me to imagine a hungry person, standing at the head of a buffet serving line, saying, "Darn it! I wish they were serving only bread and water. These other options I have to choose from aren't worth the stress they're causing me."

I've personally learned more choices available to me in my life and work equal more opportunities for my success. Conversely, fewer choices mean significantly more limited or restricted opportunities.

The worst imaginable situation is easy for me to pinpoint: having others make all or most of my choices for me. If you're not so sure, just ask those who are incarcerated, institutionalized, or physically incapacitated what their situations are like.

And here's the best part of all. When you have choices, you can choose to pursue money and power or happiness and enlightenment. It's your choice. You can choose to move forward in pursuit of an opportunity or be satisfied with where you are and what you have. Again, that's the point—it's *your* choice!

You choose your own path to success rather than being herded down a path that someone else has chosen for you when you make conscientious choices. And our job as leaders is to strive to create an opportunity-rich environment—providing more, not fewer choices—for ourselves and for our followers.

A Professional Triple Threat

The first and best way of putting yourself in a situation that affords you infinitely more choices is to become the person others can't ignore when they're seeking someone to solve their problems or answer their questions. Your best bet in becoming that person is by becoming a professional triple threat.

In baseball, a triple threat is a player who can hit, run, and throw—someone highly proficient in all three of the major aspects of the game. In life and work, a professional triple threat is an individual possessing knowledge, skills, and desire—who is adept in the three critical areas that set the stage for unprecedented personal and leadership success.

Knowledge and Understanding

Of the three elements necessary to become a professional triple threat, knowledge is probably the easiest to secure—you can acquire it through formal education, training, experience, coaching, or mentoring.

But please be careful. Don't fall victim to the myth that just because you have a college degree, some sort of professional certification, significant years of experience, or a well-known mentor that you've somehow gained adequate knowledge to be successful. It's just not that easy. Author Mark Twain put his own humorous spin on the knowledge issue when he wrote, "It's not what you don't know that gets you in trouble. It's what you know for sure that ain't so." Twain's observation dovetails nicely with the old saying that "he knows just enough to be danger-ous"; that is, knowledge can be perilous if we don't possess a clear understanding of how to use what we know appropriately.

For example, it's common knowledge that some of our followers are motivated and some aren't. In Chapter 7, "Why People Do What They Do," I introduced you to the corner-stone concept to help you better understand the why and the what that drive all human behavior. Remember—*all human behavior is directed toward the satisfaction of needs.* Recall that while we may know that our employee, Sally, is interested in being promoted, we also need to understand which of Sally's needs this promotion will satisfy (e.g., the need for a salary increase, the need for more prestige within the industry, or the need to have unobstructed opportunities to implement her ideas). It's critical for you to know and understand these things—because only then can you work to keep Sally moti-vated by helping her satisfy her most pressing needs.

Skills and Application

The second element necessary for professional triple threat development is skill, which differs from knowledge. I'm sure you know people who have high degrees of knowledge, yet can't seem to do anything practical with that knowledge.

Conversely, great numbers of people can do phenomenal things but often don't understand the big picture. An animal trainer can teach a monkey to do amazing tricks if she pitches the animal a peanut (reward) at the right time. However, the monkey has no concept of why the trick is important or valuable.

Unfortunately, employees in many organizations are similarly trained and conditioned. They're rewarded for their skills (behavior or performance) but are not adequately informed as to why or how those skills are important to the organization's overall objectives.

But take heart. You can be sure that you're successfully mastering the skills of leadership (or any other job, for that matter) if you can take your skills and apply them appropriately with clear knowledge and understanding as to what you specifically wish to accomplish. You don't wander willy-nilly through your day. You approach your day, for instance, understanding the need to apply the communication skills you possess to root out the underlying cause of ongoing conflict between two of your followers. And when you apply them well, your skills become valuable building tools in constructing your long-term leadership success.

Personal Desire and Commitment

The third element of becoming a professional triple threat is personal desire (commitment), which is frankly the most important of the three. I've known individuals—and I'll bet you have, too—who possess both knowledge (understanding) and skills (application) in significant measure yet who remain woefully unsuccessful compared to their potential. Remember the story of the unsuccessful manager I used to kick off this chapter? How can it be that someone with such promise and years of opportunity falls so short?

Plain and simple, these individuals lack the personal desire (commitment) to forge ahead while employing their knowledge and skills toward the opportunities available to them. Their attitude regarding continuous growth and personal development often—well, it stinks. They're satisfied with the status quo. They're not interested in learning or doing more. They've settled into a comfortable zone, choosing to employ most of their energies in an effort to stay right where they are, strenuously resisting most attempts to move forward.

Please understand that I'm not saying these are bad people. It's just that their personal desire—if it ever existed—has been diminished significantly, if not extinguished completely.

Now, chances are that if you told them that, they wouldn't agree. They'd most likely counter with a dozen reasons why the world is out to get them. Why the training that had been available to them was inconvenient. Or why the committee they had been invited to serve on or even chair would've simply required too much time, without adequate guarantee of some future, personal benefit. The truth is, whether they recognize or admit it or not, they've actually been blocking their own success path due to their lack of personal desire (commitment) to be successful.

"I Should've Bought That Farm"

When I was a young boy, I loved riding around the countryside in a pickup truck with my father. We traveled frequently to and through Farmersville, Kentucky, the small, rural community where my dad was born and raised. Time and again, while passing through, my dad would point out a specific parcel of land and comment, "I should've bought that farm when your mother and I first got married. It could've been ours for almost nothing then." Upon delivering those words, his voice would usually drift off, giving way to silent, wistful thinking.

My dad never bought that farm. And I'm sure he never stopped regretting that fact. My dad's gone now, but I still think about those truck rides. And almost every time I pass that farm, I remember his words. They're as clear in my mind today as they were 50 years ago when I first began hearing them: "I should've bought that farm. . . ."

Commonsense Success Choice #1: If I Am to Fail, I Choose to Fail Aggressively

Those truck rides—as well as a thousand other experiences, observations, and conversations from which I've benefited throughout my life—have left their mark. In part, they've taught me the value of embracing and employing commonsense success choices in my day-to-day interactions and activities. These choices drive my thinking, my decision making, and, ultimately, my personal and professional behavior.

The first commonsense success choice I'll share is this: *If I am to fail, I choose to fail aggressively.*

This first choice took root in my consciousness years ago, while I was reflecting on my dad's lifelong regret over not buying the farm. Though there's no way of knowing for sure, I've concluded that it would've been preferable for my father to have borrowed the money, bought the farm, and ultimately lost the farm in a loan default—than endure future decades of bemoaning and lamenting what might have been.

Now, I am *not* condoning some foolish fiscal attitude that leads individuals to buy what they cannot afford, without having a legitimate plan for repaying the debts they've incurred along the way. That sounds too much like a governmental attitude, not a commonsense success choice. Leaders should always stand responsible for the commitments they make, be they financial or otherwise.

What I *am* suggesting is that the power of regret can be more debilitating over time than the embarrassment of failure. That's why I've decided that if the possibility of failure is real, yet action is necessary, I would rather fail aggressively than passively. In other words, I would rather fail trying to make something happen than while sitting on my hands watching things happen.

Humorist Mark Twain sounded a serious note when he penned the following words regarding risk and regret: "Twenty years from now you will be more disappointed by the things you didn't do than by the things you did. So throw off the bowlines. Sail away from the safe harbor. Catch the trade winds in your sails. Explore. Dream."

That's good advice. But there's one other important point that needs to be made concerning the act of "sailing from the safe harbor." Once you choose to commit to moving forward and taking action—you may be surprised to find that failure is not a given after all.

Failure is *not* inevitable. Once they commit to something, most people are able to summon up the will, imagination, and methodology to succeed. Losing the farm was not a given for my dad. I'm convinced he and Mom would have found a way to make that purchase successful. However, the failure actually came in not having the farm as a result of not doing what was necessary to secure it.

Nineteenth-century author, poet, historian, and philosopher Henry David Thoreau wrote, "If one advances confidently in the direction of his dreams, and endeavors to live the life which he has imagined, he will meet with success unexpected in common hours." I happen to agree with Thoreau. I've found that many leaders succeed in their leadership pursuits because they don't fear failure and move confidently forward, discovering success at various stages throughout the process.

Commonsense Success Choice #2: To Hit a Home Run, I Must Swing the Bat

I love baseball. But occasionally, I hear people complain that the game of baseball is boring. When I hear these comments, I have to ask them, "You didn't watch the 1991 World Series, did you?"

In October 1991, the Minnesota Twins and the Atlanta Braves squared off in the fall classic. It was the first time in Major League Baseball's history that two teams had climbed from last place in their respective divisions the year before to compete for the world championship the very next season. This best-of-seven series went a full seven games—five of which were decided by just one run, and three of which went into extra innings. Though my team (the Braves) eventually lost, it was the best World Series I'd ever watched.

Game 3 of the 1991 series is especially memorable for me. The Twins tied the game in the top of the eighth inning. My wife and I were at home watching the game together, cheering for Atlanta. But as the game wore on, stretching past midnight, Susan eventually fell asleep on the couch. I remained wide awake.

In the 10th inning, my wife began to stir. She sat up and spoke.

"What's the score?" Susan asked sleepily.

"It's tied, 4 to 4, in the 10th," I responded, almost breathlessly.

"Okay. Well, good night. I'm going to bed," she announced casually.

"What?" I almost shouted. *"Didn't you hear me? I said it's tied in the 10th!"*

"I know what you said, and I'm still going to bed," she said as she shuffled toward our bedroom, before adding sarcastically, "I'm sure you can pull 'em through without my help."

So I was left all alone in the darkened living room, with the only light emanating from the flickering television screen. I literally sat on the edge of my seat. This was Major League Baseball's premier event, featuring some of the best, most successful baseball players on the planet. I just knew something exciting was bound to happen. *Every player on both teams is capable of ending this game with a single swing of the bat,* I thought. Therefore, I sat waiting, hoping, expecting someone to hit a home run.

Then something hit me, a random thought: *What if every batter bunted?*

It was an odd thought, one I'd never entertained before. But because it was different, I stayed with the thought for awhile. It led me to an interesting leadership epiphany and, ultimately, a new personal commonsense success choice: *To hit a home run, I must swing the bat.*

The bunt is the most conservative offensive play in baseball. It entails the batter extending his bat into the path of a pitched ball for the purpose of tapping it lightly so that the ball rolls slowly in front of the infielders. Contact between the ball and the bat is fairly easy to accomplish with a bunt because the mechanics are much simpler than taking a full swing.

Baseball purists know there's a strategic place in the game for the bunt; however, it's not a very exciting play. Therefore, I found myself wondering what would happen if player after player, from both teams, inning after inning, stepped to the plate only to square around and bunt.

There are a number of things that cannot be successfully predicted. For example, you can't predict who would win or who would lose. You can't predict how the defensive team would defend such a conservative offensive strategy. You can't predict how the managers would manage under such circumstances, how the players would play, or even how the spectators would watch.

But there is one thing that can be predicted with all certainty: No one who bunts is ever going to hit a home run. The laws of physics won't allow a bunted ball to travel 300-plus feet. It's just not going to happen. To create enough force and energy to hit a home run, one must swing the bat aggressively.

And so it is with leadership success. There are certainly conservative options available to leaders. And leadership conservatism is not only wise; it's advisable under certain circumstances.

However, if a leader continuously opts for the most conservative approach—never offering alternatives to consider, never allowing subordinates to exercise independent judgment, always withholding personal opinions for fear of challenge, always resisting change regardless of the necessity—there's a lot that we can't predict.

For example, you can't predict how the marketplace will respond to this ultraconservative leadership approach. You can't predict how pleased the boss will be with this leader's status quo performance. You can't predict how professional colleagues will react to such intentional moderation. You can't predict how (or if) his followers will follow. But one thing is predictable—the leader in question is not going to lead his team (the organization) in home runs!

If we're going to make a difference and realize the success available to us, we must decide now to take a few swings. Your position as a leader requires it.

Commonsense Success Choice #3: Choosing Yes

Several years ago, I was spending some time with a professional speaking buddy of mine, Joe Calloway. Joe is a tremendous speaker and author (his books include *Becoming a Category of One: How Extraordinary Companies Transcend Commodity and Defy Comparison*), not to mention one of the most likable guys I know. I suppose one of the many reasons

I like him so is that he always gets me to think, whether he intends to or not.

During this particular conversation, Joe arrested my attention and captured my imagination. Though I've long since forgotten the context in which the line was delivered, I doubt that I'll ever forget the line itself (at least I hope I don't). Joe simply said, "If it scares me professionally, I do it."

That statement initially grabbed me as a sort of counter-intuitive musing—a thought that ended up being the opposite of what I would've expected from him. But the more I thought about it, the more I found myself agreeing with a larger principle contained in the statement.

Let's face it: Most of the things that scare us are frightening because they are new or unfamiliar to us. You'll recall that we took time to explore that concept previously in Chapter 9, "Fearsome Facts."

In the years that have passed since that conversation with Joe, that one simple thought, "If it scares me professionally, I'll do it," has morphed into another of my commonsense success choices. I call it: *Choosing Yes*.

Like most of my commonsense success choices, this one's rather simple in concept; however, it has far-reaching implications. Here's how it goes. Whenever someone approaches me with an idea, an opportunity, an invitation, a suggestion, or whatever, I immediately try to find a good, legitimate reason to say yes.

If someone says to me something like, "Phil, I'd like to discuss something with you over lunch," "I'd like to pitch an idea your way," "I'd like to get your input on how to make something work," or "I'd like to get you involved somehow,"

I immediately start trying to figure how I might say yes to this person.

Now before you start rolling your eyes and thinking that I'm a complete idiot, a pushover, someone with more time on my hands than I know what to do with, or someone so insecure that I'm afraid or unwilling to say no to anyone, take a moment to consider my reasoning. Believe it or not, there is method in my madness. I do have standards, and I'll address them right off the bat.

First, I will take the time to listen to and consider only contacts from people I know and with whom I have an established relationship or those who find their way to me from some respected, shared connection. In other words, I'm not interested in taking a call from a stranger who got my phone number from a directory and who is offering me a once-in-a-lifetime investment opportunity. I can guarantee that it would be a very short conversation.

Second, even if I know or know of them some way, I'll spend very little time with individuals who appear to be self-absorbed. You know the type. They're more interested in talking about themselves and their own personal interests than the opportunity, idea, invitation, or cause they pretend to represent. Such people turn me off, and my conversations with them are bound to end rather quickly.

Third, I have little time or patience for people to whom I've already said no. While my overarching intent is to say yes whenever possible and practical, I will say no from time to time. And if I've processed the request or inquiry and have already decided to refuse, I really don't like to have to repeat or explain it again and again. Such a circumstance

Commonsense Success

forces me to be more direct in my response than I generally prefer to be.

Finally, I will most certainly offer a quick and definitive no to anyone who brings something to my attention that does not align with my personal values, beliefs, or standards. I'm at a stage in my life where those foundations of my being are there for a reason—and they're not something I'll easily or hastily change. I'll also never say yes to any request that I determine to be in any way illegal, immoral, unethical, or highly impractical or that conflicts with my personal or professional commitments.

Other than those exceptions, I'm willing to listen and to talk. And surprisingly, I run into few conflicts concerning the limitations I listed. I try to say yes as often as possible, as I've found that it can lead to some extraordinarily exciting discoveries, adventures, and opportunities. I have a number of examples, but the most prominent one concerns my involvement in the National Speakers Association (NSA) (www.nsaspeaker.org).

I joined NSA in 1988 as a complete novice, determined to learn the art and business of professional speaking. It therefore made perfect sense to join the professional association where the best of the best professional speakers go to learn, share, and interact. I was a regular at NSA-sponsored workshops, conferences, and conventions for 14 years—learning and growing throughout.

Then in 2002, out of the blue, a longtime NSA member asked if I would be willing to serve on NSA's finance committee. Honestly, I'd never considered the possibility. I readily admitted my limited expertise in accounting and finance-related matters; but in the spirit of Choosing Yes, I agreed to serve if invited. I ended up serving a two-year term.

I learned more about NSA during the first 15 minutes of that first finance committee meeting than I'd learned in the previous 14 years of membership. Primarily, I learned what we valued by how we spent our members' money. I was involved rather than watching from the fringe.

Without belaboring this example, service on the finance committee led to an invitation to sit for election to the national board of directors. I said yes again and was elected. Serving on the board eventually led to an opportunity to join its executive committee. A few more yeses resulted in opportunities to serve as NSA treasurer and ultimately, vice president, thus leading to the presidency (2009–2010) of the National Speakers Association.

My role as NSA president required active volunteer leadership of an organization of more than 3,000 members, with a $3.5 million annual budget and a national headquarters with 13 professional staff members. My team of more than 50 volunteers, all professional speakers, planned two educational workshops (300+ attendees each) and one convention (1,500 attendees). During my presidency, I visited more than two dozen state chapters around the United States, meeting and interacting with hundreds of my professional speaking colleagues. Additionally, I traveled and visited with international professional speaking affiliates in Australia, Canada, Germany, Holland, Malaysia, Singapore, South Africa, and the United Kingdom.

I assure you, none of the opportunities listed here was etched on my career to-do list. In fact, I debated with myself (and with others, on occasion) as to the value and wisdom of saying yes at different stages. In the spirit of full disclosure, each position of service required both personal and professional sacrifice and more hours of work and travel than I care to recall. Yet, with each opportunity to lead came unforeseen and untold opportunities for both personal and professional growth and adventure. As a result, I know more today about my association, my industry, the world, and myself as a leader than I could've ever planned or orchestrated on my own. And I have new friends the world over.

Each of these opportunities began with a conscious choice to say yes or no. I chose yes more often than not. I still do—and I always will.

Former First Lady Eleanor Roosevelt once advised, "Do one thing every day that scares you." Maybe that one thing for you today is just to say yes to the next opportunity presented to you. You may find that choosing yes serves you well. It has for me.

Commonsense Success Choice #4: When I Mess Up, I Must Fess Up—Quickly

I can vividly remember our daughter Sophie's thirteenth birthday. For weeks leading up to this day, she had gone out of her way to make it abundantly clear what she wanted as a birthday gift—her first cell phone. Personally, I was solidly against it, arguing that a cell phone in the hands of an immature teenager was totally unnecessary and simply asking for trouble. The last thing we needed was an exorbitant texting bill or improper photos being sent or received.

My wife was in general agreement with me, yet she countered with the safety argument. She reminded me that unidentified perils existed out there and that Sophie needed to be able to contact us—or for us to contact her—at a moment's notice. As the professional speaker of the family, I made a very persuasive argument in support of my reasoning. But Susan is the mother, and the mother card trumps the professional speaker card every day.

Sophie's birthday fell on a Friday. Before leaving for school that morning, we opted to give her the gift. When she opened the package revealing the cell phone, a celebration broke out in the Van Hooser kitchen unlike anything I'd ever seen or imagined at that hour of the morning, or at any other hour, for that matter.

Sophie jumped and squealed, like you might expect any young teenage girl to do. She danced around the room laughing and then crying and then laughing again in rapid succession. She hugged her mother before turning her attention to me. She smothered me with an ample supply of hugs and kisses, framed with "Oh, thank you, Daddy! I love you, Daddy! Oh, you're the *best*, Daddy!" I must admit, it was an impressive display of enthusiasm and appreciation.

When Sophie finally left for school, Susan turned to me with a wry smile and that telling look. All I said was "I told you she would enjoy her gift." We both laughed.

That evening, as part of the daylong birthday celebration, our house was filled with a dozen or so 12- and 13-year-old girls. It was educational for me. For instance, I learned that such events are now called sleepovers, not slumber parties. Nevertheless, it was a big deal, with lots of activity, junk food, and giggling. Eventually, the party moved upstairs to Sophie's room, while I headed off to my own.

The next morning, I was up early, watching as the last girls stumbled out of the house one by one and into their parents' cars, each sleep deprived and far less exuberant than the night before. Eventually, our other daughter Sarah—Sophie's older sister by five years—made her appearance in the kitchen and joined me for breakfast.

"Well, they all had a big time," Sarah said nonchalantly.

"Yeah, it seems like it," I said. "I could hear them still giggling well after midnight."

"They were probably giggling about those prank calls they made," Sarah offered with a chuckle.

I stopped and put my spoon back in the cereal bowl, turning to face Sarah. Her eyes met mine. Oops.

"And what prank calls exactly are you referring to?" I asked. The cat was out of the bag.

Reluctantly, Sarah recounted the whole sordid affair. It seems that after the girls assembled in Sophie's room, they hatched an idea to make some prank calls. The primary recipient of these had been one of their middle school teachers. Calls placed to the teacher's home number went unanswered. Finally, they called the local pizza joint and placed a bogus delivery order in the teacher's name. Of course, the girls decided that the cell phone that Sophie now possessed should be used for the clandestine activity. But the scheme backfired when the teacher checked his missed call log, returned the call to the unknown number listed—and Sophie answered.

I waited for Sophie's appearance. Time was on my side.

"Good morning," I said as she entered the kitchen.

"Good morning" was her subdued reply.

"How was your party?"

"It was fine."

"Anything special go on?"

"Not really, we just watched movies, played games, and talked."

"And maybe made a few prank calls along the way?"

Sophie momentarily fell silent. She now knew that I knew. To her credit (and salvation), she denied nothing. She detailed what had transpired, explaining that it was all meant to be fun. However, she discovered that it was less fun than she had expected when, first, I confiscated her cell phone—which she had owned for a grand total of 24 hours—and put it away for the next 30 days.

Then I had Sophie call the teacher (on our landline, of course) to ask if she and I could come to his house for a personal visit later that day. He agreed. Her tears flowed before, during, and after the meeting, but she did what she needed to do—apologize personally to her teacher. The teacher accepted her sincere apology graciously.

The trip was made complete with a visit to the pizza joint. With more encouragement from dear old dad, Sophie dipped into her birthday money to pay for the large pizza that had been ordered but not enjoyed by anyone the night before. Oh yeah, she also generously tipped the delivery driver for his trouble (another suggestion from Dad). About $30 later, we made our way home.

All in all, I think it's safe to say that Sophie's thirteenth birthday party was an occasion she won't soon forget. She learned firsthand the importance of her dad's fourth commonsense success choice: *When I mess up, I must fess up—quickly*.

Okay, I realize some of you might be thinking that maybe I treated Sophie a bit too harshly. Maybe you're thinking I overreacted, that the prank call was nothing but a little bit of harmless adolescent fun.

Let me simply say that I didn't do anything to my daughter. Whatever she did, she did to herself based on her choices and actions. And yes, we all do foolish things on occasion. But the most successful of us learn how to handle the mistakes (large or small, significant or insignificant) that accompany our foolishness, as well as how to handle our successes.

What I required Sophie to do was not for my good, but for hers. You see, I learned long ago that the best policy when you mess up is to fess up—and to do so quickly and publicly. The lesson is so important I didn't want my daughter to risk missing the opportunity of learning it at the tender age of 13—as opposed to having to learn it at the hardened age of, say, 30. And I'm proud to announce that she handled herself well under the circumstances. Even her teacher said so.

One More Foundational Concept

While we're discussing mistakes—which all leaders are bound to make, again and again—I want to be sure to share one more foundational concept critical to commonsense leadership success. Here it is: To earn others' trust, one must take responsibility—quickly and publicly—for one's own actions.

As for mistakes made along the way, people can and will forgive what they can imagine themselves having done. However, they can be expected to have tremendous difficulty forgiving what they cannot imagine themselves having done.

This concept is foundational. It bears reading again and again.

You—really, everyone—will make mistakes. Personal and professional screwups are inevitable. When they occur, you must certainly seek forgiveness and provide restitution. But regarding these mistakes—be they large or small, significant or insignificant—long-lasting effects and memories can be negated based on how and when we respond to them.

In the previous chapter, I made the following statement: The act of apologizing is one of the most powerful tools available to leaders, yet unfortunately, it's one of the most seldom used. For those proactive leaders willing to use an apology when appropriate, you should know that a good apology consists of four foundational elements:

1. Acknowledgment of the offense must be quick and public.

2. A plausible explanation should be offered (if appropriate).

3. Express evident and sincere shame or regret.

4. Make provision for some sort of reparation or restitution.

It's safe to say that we're all going to mess up. But if we fess up and take appropriate action, our leadership success might be delayed—but not derailed entirely.

Conclusion

A Conclusion Isn't a Conclusion

As an author, this work represents my fifth published book. As a professional speaker, I've presented more than 3,500 speeches and training programs to professional audiences in 14 countries on six of the world's seven continents. Based solely on my body of work, some would assume that I would know better than most how to appropriately *conclude* a book or speech, considering the practice I've had.

But the truth—as many people before me have found—is that the conclusion continues to be one of my biggest professional challenges. Why? Because, in reality, I know I'm nowhere close to being finished dissecting and exploring this important subject: personal leadership and what *Leaders Ought to Know* about it.

By definition, a *conclusion* is the "last part of something" or the "final summation." But for me to embrace those definitions would be to imply that what *Leaders Ought to Know* is now sufficiently complete—to state that I've already shared everything you need to know on the topic. And that is not even close to reality.

Reading about and studying the act of leading is not the "last part of something"; rather, it's the beginning of what can be—or at least a mere water break in a continuing leadership endurance race.

As for "a final summation," traditional conclusions can quickly become monotonous by way of the old "tell 'em what you told 'em" philosophy. French winner of the Nobel Prize in Literature André Gide once wrote, "Everything that needs to be said, has been said. But since no one was listening, everything must be said again."

I'm not quite as pessimistic as Monsieur Gide, as I trust you've been listening throughout this book. Therefore, I'll resist the temptation to chew my cabbage twice, trusting instead that you've gleaned from this work the nuggets most appropriate for you and your current or anticipated leadership circumstance.

Congratulations to You

So rather than repeat myself, I'll congratulate you. Specifically, I congratulate you for staying with this book to its natural conclusion. That may not seem like a big deal to you right now, but your willingness to read, consider, and apply this book's message represents a progressive step forward in your continuing journey toward personal leadership success.

"A man's accomplishments in life are the cumulative effect of his attention to detail." Those words, spoken by President Dwight D. Eisenhower's Secretary of State John Foster Dulles, echo the commonsense refrain found throughout this book; that is, if you take care of the little things (attention to detail), common sense teaches us that the big things will generally take care of themselves. However, if we ignore or fail to take care of the details, they tend to grow and eventually fester into the big things (cumulative effect) that require considerable attention, time, and effort—all of which ultimately disrupts our leadership labors.

Leaders Are Readers—or Are They?

According to a 2007 Associated Press Poll conducted by IPSOS Public Affairs, 27 percent (one of every four) of the general population of Americans surveyed admitted to not having read *even one book* over the course of the prior year (2006). Surprised? Keep reading.

Of the 73 percent who said they *had* read a book, 41 percent had read 1 to 5 books in the previous year, 31 percent had read 6 to 15, and 27 percent had read more than 15 books.

It's also enlightening to consider the types of books that were read. That same AP/IPSOS poll listed a sampling, by category (percentage of people reading in parentheses), which included:

The Bible or other religious texts (64 percent)

Popular fiction (54 percent)

Nonfiction history books (54 percent)

Nonfiction biographies (48 percent)

Mystery or thriller novels (48 percent)

Romance novels (21 percent)

Business/finance (4 percent)

Self-help/self-improvement (3 percent)

If these numbers are to be believed, then it follows that a random sample of 100 managers and supervisors might reveal that 27 of them hadn't cracked a book of any kind during the previous 12 months (and possibly longer).

Of those same 100 managers and supervisors, 73 might lay claim to having read at least *one* book—from *any* category—in the year prior. Of course, we might find upon closer inspection that those books didn't include anything directly related to the work these managers and supervisors do every single day. In fact, the poll numbers would indicate that at a rate of only 3 or 4 percent (for self-help/self-improvement and business/ finance), *fewer than 3* of those 73 managers and supervisors actually read a book that might help them directly with the personal or professional challenges they're bound to encounter in their work.

Leaders Are Doers—or Should Be

Therefore, it bears repeating: congratulations once again on being one of that rare breed of leaders who has committed time and effort to advancing your leadership skills and broadening your leadership perspective.

As I've counseled my children for years—and mentioned several times throughout this book—the most successful among us are not necessarily the smartest, the strongest, the oldest, the best educated, the most experienced, the most attractive, or the most outgoing. The ones who actually experience the most success in their chosen endeavors are those who do the things consistently that the unsuccessful among us could have done—and probably *should* have done—but consciously and intentionally chose not to do.

I've said it again and again throughout this book: Leadership success is a choice—one to identify and to act on. As English philosopher and physician John Locke put it, "The actions of men are the best interpreters of their thoughts." If you really want to be a successful leader, it's imperative that you take action—*do something*.

So what actions might you choose to take right now?

- Review *Leaders Ought to Know* again, right away, capturing specific takeaways for inclusion in your own personal leadership journal. And if you don't have one yet:

- Begin your own personal leadership journal. This can serve as a repository for valuable leadership ideas, techniques, quotes, anecdotes, books, articles, contacts—the possibilities are endless. (I have personally benefited from having created, utilized, and added to such a document for the past 30 years. At the end of my career, I intend to gift it to my children and grandchildren as my professional legacy. You might consider doing something similar.)

- Establish one to three specific leadership goals to accomplish within the next 90 days. Start creating a strategy for the completion of those goals today. Remember American inventor Thomas Edison's admonition to all of us, "The value of an idea lies in the using of it."

- Share what you've learned and what you're doing with someone close to you as soon as possible, as this will help to secure your personal commitment.

- The very best way to learn anything is to teach it. The very best leadership growth strategy? Each one, teach one.

- If you're in a role that allows you the opportunity to coach, mentor, or direct other developing leaders, have your followers or mentees read this book as a personal growth activity.

- As a debriefing exercise, invest time in discussing this book's content and message with your followers or mentees—as well as how they can best apply it for their own leadership success.

- Make a gift of this book to a recent high school or college graduate who possesses leadership potential. Because this gift represents your interest in that person, they will likely never forget that you gave it to them.

"I Wish Buster Was Here"

I was a young human resources professional attending the first retirement party of my career. I'd been invited to the event organized to honor one of our company's most popular managers at the completion of his stellar career of more than 30 years. Family, friends, and many professional colleagues had gathered in significant numbers for the special festivities, which included a social hour and dinner, followed by a formal roasting of the honoree.

The roast featured a number of friends and colleagues who knew the honoree best—some for the entirety of his career. They shared illustrative stories and vignettes, each carefully chosen for their humor and insight into the man of honor's character. The stories provided levity, sandwiched between heartfelt comments alluding to what a tremendous leader this gentleman had been. Toward the end of the program, he himself stepped to the lectern to offer his closing remarks.

He began with a few fun-loving verbal jabs in response to the good-natured ribbing he had just taken. But his comments soon turned reflective and a bit sentimental. "Thank you all for coming out tonight to celebrate this occasion with me. I've thoroughly enjoyed this evening and I appreciate every kind word and deed that has come my way. But I must admit that I stand here with bittersweet feelings. Sweet, in that I'm surrounded by some of the most special people in my life. Bitter, in that I realize that the time I'll be able to spend with many of you will be greatly curtailed as a result of my retirement."

His comments then took a reflective turn. "As I think back on my career, I must admit that I wish our old friend Buster was here to see this."

Around the room, senior employees nodded their heads in agreement. They remembered Buster. I'd never met him. By the time I was hired, Buster had already retired and passed away. But I had heard many stories of Buster and his legendary leadership exploits. At the very mention of his name, it was obvious his memory was still alive in the minds and hearts of many.

"Some of you may not realize it, but Buster hired me 31 years ago this month. I was young and unproven.

Therefore, he took a big risk in hiring me. So I worked hard and tried to do the best I could. But I will never forget what Buster told me on my first anniversary with this company.

"I was at my work station as usual that morning when Buster walked up and put his arm around my shoulder. He looked at me and asked, 'Son, do you know what today is?' Honestly, I didn't know what he was talking about at first. But then he reminded me that it was my service anniversary date. I couldn't believe he remembered, but he did. He kept talking. 'Today is your first anniversary with the company,' he said. 'One year ago today, you started here. Today, I want to congratulate you. This isn't an easy place to work. Much is expected of us here, and a person's first year can be really challenging. But I want you to know that I've been watching you during the past year and you've continuously impressed me. I'm convinced that you're something special. I'm convinced that you're going to do special things here and you're going to have a tremendous career. My only wish is that I'll still be around when you retire, because I know what you'll accomplish between now and then will be phenomenal. I'm glad I had a little part in it.'"

I glanced around the room and saw heads nodding everywhere. Many smiled knowingly. A few dabbed at the corners of their eyes with their napkins.

The honoree concluded his remarks by adding, "I've never forgotten Buster's words. They were inspirational to me then, and they've continued to be throughout my career."

I remember sitting in the audience that night thinking, *I wonder how many people this guy has met through his professional interactions over the past 31 years—it must be hundreds, at least. And I wonder how many conversations he's had with those he's met—it has to be thousands, maybe tens of thousands! Why would he think of just one guy and that one particular conversation on this most special occasion?*

I was too young and inexperienced to fully understand and appreciate the breadth and magnitude of his comments on that occasion three decades ago. But today, more than 30 years later, I understand perfectly the impact that a true leader can have.

Today, I get it. And I hope you get it, too.

Because it's something *Leaders Ought to Know*.

You've just finished *Leaders Ought to Know.*

The book is the start. What's your next step?

If you want to build on what *Leaders Ought to Know*, consider these additional options:

1. Customized on-site *Leaders Ought to Know* training led by Phillip Van Hooser

2. Convenient online *Leaders Ought to Know* training developed by Phillip Van Hooser

Leaders Ought to Know gives leaders the skills and confidence to take your organization to the next level. Our in-depth leadership development options teach the critical skills every leader should know—and master—to maximize leadership performance and gets results!

For more information and custom quotes, please contact: info@ LeadersOughtToKnow.com

Connect with Phillip Van Hooser at:

www.VanHooser.com

www.LeadersOughtToKnow.com

Twitter: @philvanhooser

Facebook.com/philvanhooser

LinkedIn.com/in/phillipvanhooser

YouTube.com/philvanhooser

phil@vanhooser.com

+1-270-365-1536